INTRODUCTION

indication that he was a man dedicated to truthful work. Even if he were not, other people knew Macrina. In his time and culture, Nyssen was taking a risk to write about a woman as he did, and there were powerful people nearby who would have been only too happy to use any dubious claims in The Life of Macrina as a basis to attack his credibility and reputation. It is very unlikely that he wrote whole-cloth fabrications. That said, there is ultimately no way to know when the words Nyssen ascribes to Macrina came, verbatim, from her lips. Sometimes there seems to be a basis to speculate that aspects of Nyssen's work reflect his own input, and there are passages that seem especially likely to represent Macrina's own expression. Beyond this, there is simply Macrina as told by Nyssen. We must accept that Nyssen's writings contain only those aspects of Macrina's life and teaching that he understood and, presumably, only theology with which he agreed. That said, it makes sense that he would have understood and agreed with much of what she thought—about eight years younger than Macrina, he was instructed and formed with and by her, and they spent their lifetimes in close contact and communication.

Another thorny issue arises from the highly gender-stratified nature of ancient society. In those days, women had no personal rights. They lived by the choices, and under the supervision, of their fathers and then their husbands. Modesty equated to virtue, and women's voices were rarely heard in public places. Some authors question whether or to what extent Macrina's brothers, as men in that culture, could have accurately seen or portrayed her experience and thoughts. While this is an interesting question, and one that could open complex and multi-faceted discussion beyond the scope of the present volume, Macrina's brothers did express views of women that were uncommonly positive and affirming for their time. Nyssen's preserved writings convey deep personal affection for her and profound respect for her wisdom. Indications of such feelings can be found in Basil's letters also, as will be discussed below and in chapter 8. Macrina's brothers were men of their time and culture, certainly; however, my study of their work has led to the impression that these men genuinely revered and tried to honor their sister, both in their words and in their silences. My working theory is that, whatever their limitations in conveying her charism, the ancient authors tried to present accurate accounts of events and genuine perceptions of Macrina.

One more thorny issue pertains to dating events in the story of Macrina and her family. Readers should keep in mind that most of the dates mentioned in the narrative are uncertain to one degree or another. Not only do differing dates occur in various sources, but conflicting accounts of facts and sequences of events are also easy to find. I have tried to rely on well-researched, up-to-date sources. I am especially grateful and indebted to the remarkable work of Anna Silvas in providing comprehensively researched and clearly explained historical information, as well as beautiful, respectful, insightful, and incisive translations of the ancient materials.

Basil the Great and Macrina the Younger

Much has been made of the fact that her brother Saint Basil the Great does not mention Macrina by name in any of his extant writings, and none of his hundreds of preserved letters are addressed to her. Some authors have read this as a sign of a rift between brother and sister, and even speculated about Basil's motives, ranging from sibling rivalry and family dysfunction to pride and personality conflicts.[1] These interpretations are problematic for several reasons.

First, it is important to note that Basil's surviving letters are mostly his business correspondence as a church and city leader. He wrote to people to ask them to do things, to argue points of theology, to plan meetings, and so on. He does not mention *any* of his family members unless they are specifically relevant to the business matter he is addressing. He never mentions his brother Naucratius. He refers to his father only in the context of advocating for a reduced tax assessment for a family retainer, and then only to mention a business arrangement set up by Basil the Elder for the benefit of this retainer. He refers to his mother, though never by name. He names his brother Peter only once, and he never mentions any of his sisters by name.

Second, Basil's extant writings are not a complete collection of what he wrote in his life. As Silvas notes, the fact that we do not have letters between Basil and Macrina does not prove that they never existed—there are other cases in which letters that clearly existed have been lost.

Third, caution is warranted in projecting the social meaning that would apply in contemporary, Western culture onto the actions of people in ancient times and of a different culture. In his own time and context, Basil's consistent non-mention of family members may not have suggested disregard or estrangement. He and his family were part of a culture that had

1. Van Dam, *Families and Friends*, 21–24.

INTRODUCTION

endured wave after wave of occupying empire, a people that had survived invasions and aggressions, attempts at domination and exploitation by outsiders for thousands of years. Under these pressures, the people of central Asia Minor developed toughness, loyalty, courage, resourcefulness, and caution. Their society and customs were shaped by determination to maintain the greatest possible autonomy, integrity, and independence despite the long series of world powers that marched in to rule over them.

These qualities were, perhaps, magnified in Macrina and her siblings. As chapter 1 will tell, their parents were survivors of the Great Persecution, a deeply traumatized generation who knew, and taught their children, that sudden, violent, catastrophic change absolutely *could*, and at any time *might*, happen. Not only were the lessons of their parents' lives vivid in their own awareness, Macrina and Basil lived in times of rapid and intense political/religious change and upheaval, which will be touched upon here and there in the pages ahead, especially the story of Basil's fearless show-down with an emperor in chapter 8. Christians had been alternately accepted and persecuted over more than two centuries. Just fifteen years before Macrina was born, the latest persecution ended when the Edict of Milan legalized the religion. There were still powerful people poised to bring new persecutions upon Christians if they had the chance. Indeed, in 361 CE, early in Basil's career, when he and Macrina were in their thirties, Julian the Apostate became emperor and set in motion an aggressive program to return the Roman Empire to Paganism. Julian encouraged anti-Christian violence, burned Christian books, and used administrative moves to disempower, humiliate, and burden Christian leaders. Julian's hostility focused especially on Basil's home city of Caesarea, where he renovated a shrine to a Pagan spirit. When the shrine was destroyed by locals, he retaliated by stripping Caesarea's rank as a city, confiscating three hundred pounds of gold that belonged to the church, enrolling its clergy on the roster of bureaucrats obliged to serve the Roman governor, and imposing additional taxes on Christians. His actions raised fierce opposition among the people of the region and Julian was, in the end, unable to enforce his orders. He left the area rather quickly, but on his way out, he announced that Basil and his close friend Gregory of Nazianzus (Nazianzen) were to be regarded as enemies of the Empire and told them that, like the Cyclops leaving Odysseus and his men trapped in the cave, they could be sure that he would be coming back to eat them.[2]

2. Van Dam, *Kingdom of Snow*, 100–101.

INTRODUCTION

Basil was a man with a family history of trauma who lived on the frontlines of the struggle for faith and local autonomy. He had every reason for the greatest caution regarding the powers of the realm, and little basis to trust *anyone*. His official silence about his family members may have reflected protective loyalty rather than disrespect or difficulty in giving credit to others. Perhaps he held a shield of privacy over his family, writing least of those he held closest to his heart.

Finally, and perhaps most significantly, far from disrespecting Macrina, Basil's silence honored the essence of her vocation. Her charism was a spirituality of inner participation in divine grace made possible through hiddenness. She chose to be unseen so that she could pray—and perform all her acts—before and in-relation-to God, without being influenced by the perceptions of other people. Not to be known was her fame, as her brother Nyssen put it.[3] She wanted no attention focused on herself. Her brothers could not have written about her during her lifetime without violating the sanctuary of her hiddenness. Nyssen wrote about her only after her death. Basil never had the chance to do so because he died just before Macrina. Never-the-less, Basil's esteem of Macrina is written between the lines. As Silvas points out,

> Several [of Basil's] texts refer to Macrina implicitly, especially when Basil defends and praises women in the ascetic life or depicts the ideal cenobitic community. Basil in his time was the great champion of feminine virginity and asceticism as a lifelong vocation in the Church, and in this context we should keep in mind the degree to which the example of Macrina informs his writing . . .[4]

---

3. Gregory of Nyssa, *The Life of Saint Macrina*, (trans. Corrigan), 30.
4. Silvas, *Saint Macrina the Younger*, 69

1

Pearl Beyond Price

"The kingdom of heaven is like a merchant in search of fine pearls; on finding one pearl of great value, he went and sold all that he had and bought it." (Matt 13:45–46)

AROUND THE YEAR 330 CE, in the city of Neocaesaria in the ancient Roman province of Pontus (now central Turkey), a girl called Macrina was growing up in a family made up of her grandmother, mother, father, and eight (living) sisters and brothers. Depending on the source and tradition one reads, between five and eight members of this remarkable family are now honored as saints. The girl is now known as St. Macrina the Younger and her grandmother as St. Macrina the Elder. Her little brothers included St. Basil the Great and St. Gregory of Nyssa, two of the Cappadocian Fathers—early Christian theologians who were among the most important voices in articulating the Christian faith as it is still known and practiced today. Macrina's youngest brother, St. Peter II of Sebasteia, worked alongside her throughout her life. Another brother, Naucratius, chose a life of radical simplicity, service, and dedication to God. Macrina's parents are also considered saints in some traditions.

Young Macrina and her family of saints lived in a singular and beautiful place and at one of the great turning points in history: they lived at just the moment when Christianity—until then an illegal and often forcefully suppressed movement—was taken as the officially sanctioned religion of the Roman Empire.

Pontus and the neighboring province of Cappadocia were in Asia Minor, on the high Anatolian plains. Surrounded by mountain ranges, at elevations around 3,500 to 4,000 feet above sea level, this is a region of cold, snowy winters and hot, dry summers. The Anatolian landscape is marked by striking formations of pale, soft volcanic tufa rock which are, in some places, erosion-lathed to fanciful shapes like sandcastles, fairy chimneys, and ice cream cones. Captivating in their own right, these natural stone figures stand among, and sometimes contain, human-made dwellings that are sculpted right in the tufa rock. There are houses, gathering rooms, stables, storerooms, and even underground cities made in and of the very hills themselves.

Although not yet carved in the time of ancient Rome, stunning churches were cut in the stone in later centuries. A cliff face is chiseled to the shape of a stone cathedral front, with massive pillars, arched windows, and a door leading right into the hill. Inside, the rock is hollowed, the interior spaces cut from the hill's stone center. There are also houses that seem to grow out of the hills, with rooms dug into the hill-rock on one side and built out with mortared stone on the other. Built wall seamlessly continues the line of carved hill, forming beautiful and arresting dwellings. To foreign eyes, these hill homes are enchanting, irresistible, like something from a fairy tale, a myth, or a fantasy film set—a Near Eastern setting of *The Hobbit* perhaps. The stories contained in their history, however, are real as the rock itself and filled with more wonder, meaning, horror, and awe than any fiction.

Scattered over large areas, many of the stone-carved habitations are now abandoned, though some are still occupied, and a few have been made over into hotels for tourists who come to see these World Heritage Site cultural treasures. Sightseers today can ride in hot air balloons over the sculpted hills, cupped valleys, winding rivers, and fertile basins where the people of ancient Cappadocia and Pontus built their more conventional mortared-stone villages and tended their goats and sheep, pigs and cattle, camels and donkeys, and their fine and famous horses. In the tufa rock houses one can see where they kept colonies of pigeons and bees, and in the surrounding lands where they farmed fields of grain and terraced the hills to grow vineyards, orchards, and vegetable gardens.

These people, already steeled by their environment, also endured wave after wave of invaders who tried to control them and extract the rich resources of their land: over two millennia leading up to the time of Christ, they had been under the rulership of a succession of empires—the Hittites, Phrygians, Persians, Greeks, and Romans. Among these outsiders, people of the region earned a reputation for toughness. As Raymond Van Dam quotes in his book Kingdom of Snow, one epigram describing these people read, "A venomous viper bit a Cappadocian. The viper died."[1]

In ancient times, a plurality of religious traditions, indigenous to the area and brought in by various occupying empires, coexisted in Asia Minor—Greek polytheism, Zoroastrianism, and the cults of Anatolian and Persian gods. When Rome took control of the area, it brought its own pantheon of gods and its deified emperors, but Rome generally tolerated the gods and rituals of people in its client kingdoms and imperial provinces, so long as these local religions did not tend toward insurgency or undermine the official pagan religion of the empire.

Between about 50 and 200 CE, a strange new upstart faith began making waves. Instead of a glorious and useful warrior God who could lend divine muscle to destroy enemies, this faith offered an unarmed God-man who allowed himself to be killed in the most miserable and humiliating manner possible, demonstrating and teaching transcendence of the needs to dominate, win, and own. People gathered to tell and to hear stories of the wonder and the potency of this new faith. According to the ancient texts, these people saw their faith cure disease, feed the hungry, quiet storms, bring down despots, and raise up the poor. Hearing of these miracles, some people wanted to convert, but for the ancient people, conversion was a radical and dangerous choice. Not only would a conversion change daily life, social standing, and prospects, but, depending on the shifting political winds, conversion might just get you and your family dispossessed, exiled, tortured, or killed. Christianity, as it turned out, was a problem for the Roman rulers: it challenged the divinity of the emperor and the validity of the pagan beliefs of the ruling majority. Worse, Christians engaged in acts of resistance such as refusing to take part in pagan sacrifices that were expected of everyone in the community. This led to waves of violent persecution, including the infamous spectacles in which Christians were thrown into the arena to fight to the death against hungry lions.

But believers in the new faith were undeterred. Christ promised to fulfill all their needs and open the way to an unending peace and freedom, transcending even the power of death. For these ancient followers of the gospel, death as a martyr was the ultimate act of faith, and so, despite

---

1. Van Dam, *Kingdom of Snow*, 14.

everything that was done to them, they continued to worship, to live and tell bold stories of the works of God, and to welcome converts.

Between Jesus' death and Macrina's life, periods of intense persecution were separated by times of greater toleration when Christians could worship openly, preach publicly, and build churches. About a century before Macrina's birth, during one of these more friendly periods, a youth named Gregory lived in her own home city of Neocaesaria. When he was a young man, Gregory traveled down to Judaea (modern Israel) to study with Origen Adamantius (184–253 CE). An orator, writer, and teacher, Origen was internationally known for his brilliance, his clarity, and his ability to ignite enthusiasm in hearers. One student wrote about listening to Origen lecture:

> It was like a spark falling in our deepest soul, setting it on fire, making it burst into flame within us. It was, at the same time, a love for the Holy Word, the most beautiful object of all that, by its ineffable beauty attracts all things to itself with irresistible force, and it was also love for this man, the friend and advocate of the Holy Word.[2]

Origen's gifts and ideas made him so notorious and controversial that officials of the church and of the empire became concerned about him. At various times he was exiled from his hometown of Alexandria (on the northern coast of Egypt), ordered back to Alexandria, sent on journeys to other destinations, and threatened with arrest. During a period of favor, he founded a school in Caesarea Palestinae where his teaching drew followers including Gregory of Neocaesaria. Later he had to go into hiding in the homes of protectors (see Appendix 1).

Among the things young Gregory learned at Origen's school was an influential and controversial approach to the reading and interpretation of Scripture. Origen taught that Scripture can be interpreted on three levels: the letter (a literal reading), the soul (roughly a psychological/moral or figurative reading), and the spirit (an allegorical reading of Scripture as a symbolic account of the mysteries of Christian faith). He believed the Holy Spirit provided Scripture that could be read on each of these different levels so that its teaching could be accessed by the whole range of humanity and by people at all stages of the journey of faith. The literal reading, he taught, is useful when we want or need uncomplicated instruction. The figurative and allegorical readings invite us, as we are ready and able, to engage more

---

2. McGuckin, *Westminster Handbook to Origen*, 18.

deeply in seeing the lessons of wisdom and the mysteries of faith "hidden beneath the veil of the literal text of ancient scriptures."[3]

Origen's method for accessing the soul and spirit through Scripture was not unlike the practice many know today as Lectio Divina (Divine Reading): he held Scripture in his mind with a prayerful gaze, ready for the words to open into spiritual meanings that were not immediately obvious. Origen wrote a letter to Gregory explaining this method:

> While you study these divine works . . . knock at that which is closed in them, and it shall be opened to you by the porter, of whom Jesus says, 'To him the porter opens.' [John 10:3] While you attend to this divine reading seek aright and with unwavering faith in God the hidden sense which is present in most passages of the divine Scriptures. And do not be content with knocking and seeking, for what is most necessary for understanding divine things is prayer.[4]

After studying with Origen, Gregory returned to Neocaesaria where he converted almost every person in the city from pagan to Christian through his teaching, preaching, and live demonstrations of faith in action. He became known as St. Gregory the Wonder Worker or St. Gregory Thaumaturgus. According to legend, his faith was so powerful that it could heal people, subdue demons, reverse floods, and dry up lakes. He moved great stones by faith alone and led the people of Pontus to build a new church which, about seventy years later, was the only building left standing after an earthquake reduced the rest of the city to rubble. Thaumaturgus led the Christian community of Neocaesaria until his death in 270 CE. His ministry was carried forward by his followers, including the family of Macrina's father, Basil the Elder. Indeed, Macrina's grandmother, St. Macrina the Elder, may have worshipped in Thaumaturgus's congregation; she was formed in the faith by his teaching or that of leaders trained by him.

Christians thrived in Pontus and Cappadocia until everything changed in 303 CE. Possibly persuaded by the Cappadocian governor Maximus Galerius, in February 303 the Roman Emperor Diocletian issued an edict outlawing Christianity throughout the empire, commanding that Christian churches everywhere be leveled to the ground, Scriptures destroyed by fire, and Christians killed or banished. With this, the last and "Great" persecution of Christians by the Roman Empire began.

---

3. McGuckin, *Westminster Handbook to Origen*, 49.
4. Origen, *Complete Works, Letter to Gregory*, 379.

Governor Galerius was a man on-the-move in the Roman power hierarchy, and he was, by all accounts, extraordinarily ruthless, violent, and cruel. He set about enforcing the edict of persecution swiftly and decisively. Christians in his provinces were turned out of their homes, stripped of their belongings, and publicly tortured and killed. Lands, livestock, buildings, and belongings were taken from rich and poor alike. People fled for their lives with little or nothing. They formed small bands and hid in the forests, the hills, and the volcanic tufa rock dwellings. For the next decade, these refugees continued their Christian study, prayer, and worship while Roman soldiers roamed through the region on horseback and on foot hunting for them. The fugitive faithful pooled their efforts and resources and survived as best they could. We know they hunted and gathered, maybe they grew small gardens at a distance from their encampments, possibly they were able to slip onto estates to work as laborers during times of high demand (planting, harvest, sheep-shearing), and perhaps they received help from secret sympathizers.

Among the bands of fugitive Christians were Macrina's parents and grandparents. Her mother's parents were well-to-do people, aristocrats in their Cappadocian community, owners of large estates and great herds of livestock. Macrina's mother Emmelia was born during the persecutions, around 305–309 CE, and both of her parents died in exile, leaving Emmelia an orphan among the refugees.

In the next province north, Macrina's father's family was also dispossessed and chased into hiding. Basil the Elder was perhaps eight years old when the edict of persecution was issued. His father probably died as a refugee and Basil grew to adulthood among the fugitives with his mother, Macrina the Elder.

Macrina the Elder was central in preserving the teachings and traditions of Thaumaturgus through the Great Persecution. Indeed, according to legend, she carried his relics (bones) with her through all the years in hiding. Her grandsons later wrote of how she instructed them in the faith she learned in his congregation and taught them his practice of psalmody and prayer at regular hours and in conjunction with the activities that marked the passage of each day. Rooted in ancient Judaism and carried forward by Elder Macrina's grandchildren Macrina and Basil, the practice of observing the canonical hours was built into the very foundations of Christian monastic life as it is still carried on today.

Stripped of every outward thing, the banished Christians gave shape to their days and focus to their actions by singing psalms and saying prayers upon rising, when working, when resting, at meals, and at the close of the day. They turned toward the gospel, sought union with God, and found value and meaning even in their terrible situation.

While the refugees hid and struggled to survive, Governor Galerius advanced his career in the Roman hierarchy. By the year 310 CE, through a combination of position and influence, he became emperor—the most powerful person in the world. At just about the same time, however, he was stricken with a horrible and painful disease. Historians speculate that he may have had a form of advanced bowel cancer, perhaps complicated by gangrene. His condition was hideous and extremely painful. Galerius may have thought his suffering was the revenge of the Christian God, because in 311 he issued an edict granting a greater degree of toleration to Christians. This late act of mercy, however, did not save Galerius—he died later that year.

Changes in imperial politics over the next two or three years made conditions for Christians gradually more positive until, in 313, the new emperor Constantine issued the Edict of Milan making Christianity the official Roman imperial religion. Christians could safely come out of the hills and openly worship. Beyond even this safety and freedom, Constantine also restored property to those who had been dispossessed, including both of Macrina's parents.

Basil and Emmelia did not know each other during the persecution, their families lived in different provinces, and they would have sheltered in separate refugee communities, but as their heritage was restored their histories and situations were similar. Both were blessed with health, wealth, and youth. Both were fortunate in the education they had received during their exile, and both faced enormous adjustment and steep learning as they stepped from the refugee camps to their inherited roles as heads of large estates, including property, livestock, peasants and enslaved laborers, and agricultural apparatus. It is easy to imagine that this would have been both an exciting and a daunting time. In the story ahead, we will see how Basil's mother, Macrina the Elder, provided both guidance in their new world and continuity with the life they lived in refugee communities. As their story unfolds, we will see Emmelia and Basil blessed in many more ways, especially in their children. For all these blessings, however, their greatest treasure and the defining focus of their lives was their faith.

It was in and with and for this faith that their families had risked everything and endured some of the worst things that could happen to anyone: loss and trauma, torture and humiliation, life in exile as hunted fugitives, untimely death making orphans of their children. Pain, grief, and love blazed within them. Distractions and self-involved concerns were cleared away in the extremity of their situation, and faith remained as the center and the purpose of their lives.

Meditation

Take a moment to focus. Seat yourself comfortably, feel your body resting on your chair, let your breath fill you and release again. Invite stillness within. Choose a Scripture passage if you like, perhaps Luke 18:18–30, Matt 13:44–53, Luke 22:41–44, Matt 27:26–31 and 39–51, or 1 Thess 5:16–18. One passage is enough, or choose more.

Read once focusing on the words. Read again focusing on your own response. Is there a word or phrase that affects you, resonates in you, delights or troubles you? Read once more and hold the passage in prayerful gaze. If a door of insight, emotion, or awareness should open, simply be present in what the spirit is showing you.

2

Sex, Freedom, and the Meaning of Life

"You were called to freedom, brothers and sisters; only do not use your freedom as an opportunity for self-indulgence, but through love become slaves to one another. For the whole law is summed up in a single commandment, 'you shall love your neighbor as yourself.'" (Gal 5:13–14)

MACRINA'S MOTHER, EMMELIA, WAS orphaned during the Great Persecution and spent her early years among the fugitive Christians who worked and prayed together in the hill camps and tufa rock houses. From this harsh beginning, her situation as a young woman might seem a fairy tale of good fortune—she found herself a teenage heiress with the means and position to live in luxury, marry well, and gain social prestige. Despite these great opportunities, however, Emmelia was a young woman with a very different idea for her future.

Emmelia was probably between the ages of four and nine when the Edict of Milan legalized Christianity and her family's estate was restored to her. There is little information about her guardians and mentors, but in their care she grew to be "so virtuous a person that she let herself be led by the will of God in everything."[1] In fact, she hoped to be called by God to a life wholly focused on prayer and religious devotion, a life of vowed virginity. In the face of fabulous worldly prospects, her heart's

1. Gregory of Nyssa, *Life of Saint Macrina*, 22.

desire and greatest aspiration was to renounce all else and live as a virgin philosopher of God.

If this seems a bit surprising by contemporary standards, it was truly radical in Emmelia's day. At that time, there were not yet such things as women's religious orders, there were no publicly acknowledged dedicated religious women ("nuns") to look to as role models. For a young woman in that time and place, choosing a life of vowed virginity held momentous implications, offering perhaps the greatest promise and, as we will see in the gripping ancient story retold in chapter 3, the greatest danger of any course she might set for her life.

The promise of the virgin life was extolled by ancient Christians who spoke of vowed celibacy (for both men and women) as an expression of perfect virtue, a self-emptying work of faith, and a means of approaching mystical union with the divine. Celibacy was an essential element in the form of practice that we now call *asceticism*. The word *ascetic* comes from the ancient Greek term for exercise or physical training, such as the discipline of athletes training for the Olympic games. Religious asceticism is the practice of seeking spiritual wholeness or attainment through self-discipline, simplicity, and prayerful exertions.

Asceticism was not a Christian invention. We do not know when people first developed ascetic ideas and disciplines, but one of the earliest recorded examples began about six hundred years before Jesus' birth (and perhaps one hundred years before the birth of the Buddha, although the dates are uncertain) when, in the Ganga Valley of India, a prince named Nataputta Vardhamana was born. As a young man, Prince Nataputta rejected the privileged life he was expected to live. After years of study and meditation he became a reformer and taught a system of beliefs and practices that many people found compelling. Now known as the Mahavira (Great Hero), Nataputta laid the foundations of the Jain religion, which is still practiced today.[2]

Like other people in his cultural and religious world, the Mahavira believed that death is followed by reincarnation and that, through the effects of karma, our actions in this life determine our fate in the next. While the possibility of rebirth may sound hopeful from a contemporary Western perspective, it was not welcomed by the people of ancient India—they saw reincarnation as having to go through all the toil, suffering, and grief of

---

2. Bauer, *History of the Ancient World*, 671.

living and dying again. And again. And again.³ For them, rebirth amounted to a sort of Groundhog-Day-eternal-damnation.

This outlook on life may have been influenced by the experience of living in the hierarchical caste system of ancient India. In that society, people were born into their caste, it could not be changed, and it determined their work, living conditions, and degree of privilege. The roots of the caste system go all the way back to the nomadic horse-mounted tribes that settled in India hundreds of years before the Mahavira's lifetime. These long-ago nomads sought to understand the hidden structure that organizes all things and makes the whole cosmos work with all its breathtaking synergy and beauty by studying the structure and function of the anatomical parts of people and horses. Based on the parts that give the human body its beauty and ability and the horse its elegance, power, and speed, the nomads drew inferences about whirling stars, the changing seasons, and the management of communal life. They envisioned human society as a body constructed by the gods. The castes represented parts of this body—the top priestly caste, the brahmins, were the mouth, the warrior-ruler caste, the ksatriya the arms and hands, the craftsmen and farmers or vaisya the strong thighs and legs, and the slaves or shudra the feet. It was divinely ordained: the hands must do what the mouth tells them, the legs must exert their strength to move the body where it needs to go, and the feet must work in dust and mud to bear the burden of all the rest. Each person was made as a functional unit within a greater whole, and their destiny and purpose was to fulfill that function. The idea of changing one's caste made no more sense than saying that a foot might become a mouth.

A prince born to the ksatriya caste, the Mahavira made a choice that was revolutionary in his culture and context: as a young man, he walked away from the wealth and power of his family and position. He renounced the privileges of his birth and in doing so rejected the idea that he was defined by his caste. He seems to have thought of himself not so much as the hand of a body or a functional unit within a social structure but as a soul living in relation to the possibility of greater meaning and purpose. After years of study and meditation, the Mahavira came to the conclusion that the goal of human existence is to free oneself from endless trips around the wheel of life and death by rejecting the passions of greed, lust, and appetite. Once free from these passions, we need act *only* if our actions will help us

---

3. Adamson and Ganeri, *History of Philosophy*, 36.

eliminate the personal karma that would otherwise impel us into another rebirth, another cycle of labor and pain.

Around 567 BCE, the Mahavira set out to teach the people how they could free themselves of passions and, thereby, of karmic obligations. He walked barefoot through India, practicing and teaching the principles of nonviolence (ahimsa), truthfulness (satya), abstinence from theft of any kind (asetya), detachment from all material things (aparigraha), and abstinence from sexual pleasure (brahmacharya).[4] The Mahavira and his followers, the early Jains, were known for their ascetic practices. They were celibate in order to free themselves of lust. They kept a strictly vegetarian diet as part of their practice of non-violence. They chose extreme simplicity of dress (detachment from beautiful or luxurious attire), ranging from wrapping themselves in a single white cloth, to the "sky clad" sect which renounced all clothing and lived naked.

Taking ascetic practice to its ultimate extreme, some early Jains dedicated themselves to "immobility asceticism." These people sought to free themselves from karma by trying to sit completely still until they died from thirst, hunger, or exposure.

There is no evidence that Emmelia knew about Jainism, but their story beautifully illustrates the essential questions, hopes, and problems (see Appendix 1) of ascetic practices and movements, including the ascetic inclination that the early Christians of Anatolia brought with them from their formative experience in the refugee camps of the Great Persecution. Ascetics want to clear everything else out of the way so that they can focus completely on living according to their deepest values. They want to free themselves from the labor and attention involved in satisfying physical drives and appetites, playing out emotions, or chasing social power and status. By living simply, ascetics seek freedom to devote themselves completely to doing what is good, meaningful, and ultimately important.

What we now call social justice is also imbedded in the ascetic impulse. Ascetics choose to reject status and luxury; they hold themselves above no one, strive to take no more than they truly need, and live in such a way as to benefit as little as possible from the suffering and labor of the oppressed. Ascetics focus on living their ideals. They hold out the possibility that we can all choose to embody justice; that we can at least try not to participate in social/economic systems that cause suffering and destruction.

---

4. Bauer, *History of the Ancient World*, 672.

For Emmelia and the early Christians around her, asceticism was following Jesus of Nazareth. When a rich young man wanted to know how to enter the kingdom of heaven, Jesus told him, "If you wish to be perfect, go, sell your possessions, and give the money to the poor and you will have treasure in heaven, then come, follow me" (Matt 19:21). When a scribe approached him saying, "Teacher I will follow you wherever you go," Jesus tried to prepare him for what this might mean, saying, "Foxes have holes, and the birds of the air have their nests, but the Son of Man has nowhere to lay his head" (Matt 8:20). He told his disciples, "If any want to become my followers, let them deny themselves and take up their cross daily and follow me" (Luke 9:23). When he sent the Twelve out to take his ministry to the villages, he instructed them, "Take nothing for your journey, no staff, nor bag, nor bread, nor money—not even an extra tunic" (Luke 9:3). When he spoke of what God wanted to see in nations, he talked about feeding the hungry, giving water to the thirsty, clothing the naked, welcoming the stranger, caring for the sick, and visiting those in prison and he said, "just as you did it to one of the least of these who are members of my family, you did it to me" (Matt 27:40) (see Appendix 1).

Among ancient Christians, efforts to understand and to live the teachings of Jesus were profoundly influenced by the philosophy of Plato (428–347 BCE). Plato lived in Greece roughly two hundred years after the life of the Mahavira. Like the Gospels and the Mahavira, Plato wrote of simplicity and detachment from material things as essential to the attainment of the best of human possibilities. He saw real and genuine beingness as existing at the level of ideas—mind, soul, and divine essence. Tangible, material things that we can perceive with our bodily senses are illusory and imperfect projections of this world of ideas, like images in a shadow play (see Appendix 1). According to Plato, the real being of a person is the soul/mind, while the body and worldly life are inherently flawed representations thereof. What we see, hear, smell, touch, and taste is all shadow play, and as long as we are looking at the shadows we cannot see the true nature and essence of being. Plato argued that embodied life inherently interferes with our ability to do what is truly good. Our sensations and perceptions mislead us constantly so that we can never stop doing the wrong thing so long as we are living mortal lives in the material, sensate world. He said, "That is why we should make all speed to take flight from this world to the other, and that means becoming like the divine so far as we can, and that again is to become righteous with the help of wisdom."[5]

Emmelia very likely read Plato herself and was certainly influenced by the teachings of Origen passed down through Thaumaturgus. As a thinking man and educated Greek, Origen wanted to find a way to align a compelling faith experience with the most advanced science of his time, especially the works of Plato. Origen brought Plato's conceptual framework together with scriptural interpretation to develop a rather remarkable philosophical-mystical synthesis that was to become embedded in Christian thought through the ages. He drew from Plato the idea that only through wisdom could the philosopher understand and approach the ultimate good. From Hebrew Scripture, in the Wisdom of Solomon, Origen found the insight that wisdom is the action and image of the divine: "For she [wisdom] is a breath of the power of God, and pure emanation of the glory of the Almighty. For she is a reflection of eternal light, a spotless mirror of the working of God, and an image of his goodness" (Wis 7:25a, 26). From St. Paul, Origen added the idea that Christ is the image of the invisible God (Col 1:15; Heb 1:3). Fusing Plato, the Book of Wisdom, and St. Paul together, Origen reasoned, "Wisdom has her existence nowhere else save in Him [Christ]."[6]

Reading Scripture through a Platonic lens, Origen visualized the spiritual journey as progress from a lower, fallen state to a higher, redeemed one. That is, through prayer and religious practice, we can progress from a life driven by appetite and need toward perfect union with God. Origen put it this way: "The highest good, then, after which the whole of rational nature is seeking, which is called the end of all blessings, is defined by many philosophers as follows: The highest good, they say, is to become as like God as possible."[7] What would this look like in a human being, in a human life? Once again, in a word, wisdom.

We will come back to this coalescence of Greek philosophy and Christian faith in later chapters because it contains the seed of an idea that was to grow in the very center of Macrina's practice and understanding of faith. Her brothers used the word theosis to talk about this idea—a word that means something like "to become divine," although they were using it in a mystical rather than magical sense. Theosis is the continuous and

---

5. Plato, *Theaetetus 176a–b*, 881.
6. Origen, *De Principiis I:5*, 23.
7. Origen, *De Principiis III:6*, 178.

transformative process of growing in our capacity to embody wisdom, to embody the divine.

Origen held that this divine likeness, wisdom, is a gift of God, but that we access this gift through earnest and dedicated endeavor to subordinate the passions, including emotions and the appetites and urges of the body, to the disciplines of the soul's journey (see Appendix 1). Over the centuries, there has been confusion and controversy as to some of the specifics Origen had in mind, especially about the nature and boundaries of his own ascetic practices. Indeed, during his lifetime, there was a scandalous and discrediting rumor that Origen had actually taken self-denial to the extreme of castrating himself. Scholars still debate this matter.

Whether or not Origen made himself a eunuch "for the sake of the kingdom of heaven" (Matt 19:12), both in his time and in Emmelia's, celibacy—the virgin life—was an essential aspect of placing philosophy, wisdom, and the Spirit in ascendancy over the passions and dictates of biology. Emmelia's own son Nyssen later wrote, "Virginity is the practical method in the science of Divine life, furnishing men with the power of assimilating themselves with spiritual natures."[8] He explains:

> ... this likeness to the divine is not our work at all; it is not the achievement of any faculty of man; it is the great gift of God bestowed upon our nature at the very moment of our birth ... This truth is, I think, taught in the Gospel, when the Lord says, to those who can hear what wisdom speaks beneath a mystery, that the Kingdom of God is within you (Luke 12:21). The Divine Good ... is in fact within each of us, ignored indeed, and unnoticed while it is stifled beneath the cares and pleasures of life, but found again whenever we can turn our power of conscious thinking towards it.[9]

Nyssen, like Plato and Origen, saw subordination of bodily/sexual appetites as helpful in pushing the energies of the spirit "upward" toward spiritual growth. He articulated this idea using a hydraulic metaphor:

> The human mind ... as long as its current spreads itself in all directions over the pleasures of the senses, has no power that is worth the naming of making its way toward Real Good; but once call it back and collect it upon itself ... [and] it will find no obstacle in mounting to higher things, and in grasping realities. We often see water contained in a pipe bursting upwards through this

---

8. Gregory of Nyssa, *On Virginity*, 23.
9. Gregory of Nyssa, *On Virginity*, 37.

constraining force . . . in the same way, the mind of man, enclosed in the compact channel of an habitual continence, and not having any side issues, will be raised by virtue of its natural powers of motion to an exalted love[10] (see Appendix 1).

Nyssen argues that celibacy is a practical, useful, and effective response to the challenges of embodied life. The virgin life can set us free from what he calls "the troubles of the flesh," a broad range of preoccupations and distractions in which he saw people become embroiled. Many of these are still familiar to us today: vanity or insecurity about one's appearance and attractiveness and about losing these with the inevitable changes of age; preoccupation with obtaining or moderating sexual pleasure; the emotional commitments and imperatives of marriage and parenthood; anxiety when apart from, and fear of losing, spouse or children; the devastating grief when a spouse or child dies; and all the enormous labor, responsibility, and mundane occupations of mind and body that are involved in family life.

For women, Nyssen points out, the virgin life also means freedom from the married state in which a woman "is not her own mistress, but finds her resources only in him whom wedlock has made her lord."[11] The married woman is subject to "the shameful secrets of marriage" which he says can be learned about by reading through the laws that prescribe penalties for a "strange variety of crimes."[12] Further, the female virgin is set free from the difficulties of pregnancy and the dangers of childbirth, which he describes this way: "Her time of labor comes upon the young wife; and the occasion is regarded not as the bringing of a child into the world, but as the approach of death; in bearing it is expected that she will die; and, indeed, often this sad presentiment is true."[13] In addition to all these perils, her husband might die, and then she would be subject not only to grief but to social stigma, poverty, and vulnerability. Instead of suffering in all these ways, the young woman who chooses a life of virginity can cleave to the "undying Bridegroom," and find fulfillment of "her love for the true Wisdom, which is God." [14] She can attain "spiritual union [with] the Object of the pure and heavenly love."[15]

10. Gregory of Nyssa, *On Virginity*, 23–24.
11. Gregory of Nyssa, *On Virginity*, 23.
12. Gregory of Nyssa, *On Virginity*, 18.
13. Gregory of Nyssa, *On Virginity*, 14.
14. Gregory of Nyssa, *On Virginity*, 54.
15. Gregory of Nyssa, *On Virginity*, 54.

Putting the matter in another way, Nyssen says, "We cannot be rid of the Egyptian bondage, unless we leave Egypt."[16]

The young Emmelia hoped to be called by God to do just that. Instead of capitalizing on her wealth and opportunity to pursue position and prestige as an aristocratic wife, she wanted to embrace the life of a virgin philosopher, to free herself from other involvements so that she could give all her life and time and capacity to serving and contemplating God.

Meditation

For meditation, consider the Scriptures quoted above and these passages: Matt 6:25–34, Matt 19:16–30, 1 John 2:17, or Jas 4:13–17. Choose one or as many as you like.

Read your passage once with attention to what it says. Read it a second time with attention to what is stirred within you. What word or phrase in this passage catches your attention? Try not to enter into mental debate about the passage. Instead sit with your word or phrase. What in you responds? Can you simply be present and allow your response to be present? Read the passage a third time and hold it in prayerful gaze.

---

16. Gregory of Nyssa, *On Virginity*, 22.

3

A Secret Name

"I have called your name, you are mine." (Isa 43:1)

FOR ANCIENT CHRISTIANS, THE virgin life promised a direct path to union with God, happiness and fulfillment during mortal life, and—for women—freedom from dangers and burdens unique to their roles in the marital and domestic arrangements of the time. The young Emmelia, coming of age on the family estate, hoped and wanted to be called to that life.

Even if she had discerned and chosen this to be her final calling, however, there was a problem: in the ancient Roman empire women were not considered to be independent persons. Women could not make decisions for or about themselves, own property, or transact business except in a few circumstances. Under Roman law, women were subject to their fathers until they married and then to their husbands. This was true not only in terms of economic and practical matters but also spiritually. Girls could be contracted in marriage when they were seven years old and married when they turned twelve—their futures were settled before they were old enough to understand what was being decided for them. Fathers determined whether, when, and whom their daughters would marry. A daughter was expected to make herself an attractive, gracious, and pleasing participant in her father's plans. Should she fail to do so, she transgressed law, custom, and filial duty, and such transgressions were likely to be met with a harsh and absolute zero-tolerance policy. Indeed, there was a book circulating in the ancient Christian world that told the story of a woman who was called to the virgin life and of what she suffered as a result.

The Acts of Paul and Thecla is considered an apocryphal book—although it features the apostle Paul, authorities in the third century and after did not accept it as a verified and actual account of his actions. Whether or not it gives an entirely accurate account of the words and deeds of St. Paul, however, this fascinating little book was probably written in the apostolic era. The tradition of the Roman Catholic Church holds that the life of St. Thecla followed the course described in her Acts. Furthermore, the story was well-known and regarded as genuine by many ancient Christians, including St. Gregory of Nazianzus, St. Chrysostom, St. Augustine, and Nyssen, as well as Emmelia herself.

According to her Acts, Thecla was the daughter of a city leader in Iconium, not far from Emmelia's home city of Caesarea. She was a beautiful virgin, contracted in marriage to a man named Thamyris, when the apostle Paul came to Iconium on one of his missionary trips. Thecla listened from a window inside her home while he preached to the men of the community, including her father and brothers. She was at once too modest and obedient to go out of the house to see him, and too captivated by Paul's sermons to tear herself away from her spot. "Like a spider's web fastened to the window,"[1] she stayed there for three days listening with "vast delight and prodigious eagerness."[2] Thecla felt a compelling call to leave her place in society and go to Paul to join the Jesus movement, to follow the apostle.

When Thamyris realized that Thecla no longer wanted to marry him, he gathered the magistrates, the jailer, and a mob of men with staves. They confronted Paul and charged that he was "perverting the minds"[3] of the women of Iconium and should be put to death. Paul was imprisoned, but Thecla stole out of her house at night to go to him. She used her earrings and a silver-looking glass to bribe the jail guards so that she was let into Paul's cell. There, she sat at Paul's feet while he talked to her about Christ. Thecla learned not to fear suffering but to have courage through faith.

This lesson came just in time to sustain Thecla through the trials that were about to begin. The next morning, she was brought before the governor for breaking the law by refusing to marry Thamyris. Her own mother demanded: "Let the unjust creature be burnt; let her be burnt . . . for refusing Thamyris, that all women may learn from her to avoid such practices." The governor ordered that Thecla be burned alive in the

---

1. *Acts of Paul and Thecla*, 14.
2. *Acts of Paul and Thecla*, 14.
3. *Acts of Paul and Thecla*, 18.

midst of the theater. She was stripped naked, placed on a pyre in the stadium, and the fire lit. The brush and logs blazed beneath her, but the flames never touched her. Then the skies opened and rain poured down, extinguishing the fire. Unhurt, Thecla fled and found Paul, who had been whipped out of the city, resting in a cave. She told him she wished to follow him wherever he might go.

Paul took her with him to Antioch, where there was another dramatic showdown between the will of God and the law and custom of the city with regards to Thecla's life and vocation. This time a powerful and important man named Alexander took one look at the lovely Thecla and decided he wanted her. He spoke to Paul, who said that Thecla did not belong to him. Hearing this, Alexander seized the initiative—he laid hold of Thecla and pressed himself upon her, kissing her. She cried out and tried to fight him off. She tore his cloak and knocked the crown off his head, which made him look ridiculous. People in the street laughed at him. Outraged, he took her to the governor of Antioch where she confessed that she had refused to marry Thamyris, refused Alexander's advances, tore his cloak, and knocked his crown to the ground. She was condemned to be thrown to the beasts in the city's theater.

Thecla was stripped again and put in the arena with hungry bears and lions, but a she-lion protected her. The she-lion was killed, and then Thecla saw the water pit in the arena and felt called to be baptized. She stepped into the water saying, "in thy name, O my Lord Jesus Christ, I am this day baptized."[4] The people were sure the hungry biting fish in the water would eat her, but the fish miraculously died and floated to the surface, and Thecla was protected by a ring of fire. Other wild beasts were brought to the arena, but none of them touched her.

In desperation, Alexander had a new idea. He brought in bulls and had Thecla bound with rope which was tied to one of the bulls. The bulls were then tormented with red-hot irons to their tender parts so that they would drag and trample Thecla to death. However, the ring of fire was still there, protecting her. The flames burnt through the ropes, setting her free, and she stood unharmed in the center of the arena while the bulls stormed around.

Thecla's ordeal and the series of miracles protecting her were so overwhelming that a noble woman in the audience, Trifina, a lady of royal extraction and related to Caesar, was overcome by awe and "fainted away and

---

4. *Acts of Paul and Thecla*, 34.

died."[5] At this, Alexander and the governor decided against further efforts to martyr Thecla. They had her brought up to them, and the governor asked her to explain why none of the beasts would harm her. She told them that it was because of her belief in Jesus Christ, who "is refuge to those who are in distress; a support to the afflicted, hope and defense to those who are hopeless..."[6] The governor gave Thecla her clothes and set her free, upon which:

> The women cried out together with a loud voice, and with one accord gave praise unto God, and said: There is but one God, who is the God of Thecla; the one God who hath delivered Thecla.
> So loud were their voices that the whole city seemed to be shaken; and Trifina herself heard the glad tidings, and arose again, and ran with the multitude to meet Thecla; and embracing her, said: Now I believe in the resurrection of the dead...[7]

After recovering from her trials and spending some time sharing the gospel with Trifina, Thecla went on to teach the faith and heal the sick, eventually settling in a cave on a mountain where people brought the ill and wounded to be cured. She lived peacefully in this way for many years, until her final battle for her integrity and vocation.

When Thecla was ninety years old, fearful and envious villagers decided it was time to do something about the old lady in the cave with the frightening powers. They reasoned that she would lose all divine favor if they could strip her of her virginity, so they talked among themselves: "let us procure some rakish fellows, and after we have made them sufficiently drunk, and given them a good sum of money, let us order to them to go and debauch this virgin, promising them, if they do it, a larger reward."[8]

The drunken gang arrived at Thecla's retreat and announced their plan to rape her. She told them that they would not be able to do this, but they took hold of her by force. While they held her, she prayed and God responded: "Then a voice came from heaven, saying: Fear not, Thecla, my faithful servant, for I am with thee."[9] A great stone opened and the voice of God told her to enter the stone. She walked into the opening, and the stone closed behind her, leaving only a scrap of her veil caught where the sides of the stone sealed shut. The men stood astonished and powerless to do

---

5. *Acts of Paul and Thecla*, 35.
6. *Acts of Paul and Thecla*, 36.
7. *Acts of Paul and Thecla*, 37.
8. *Acts of Paul and Thecla*, 43.
9. *Acts of Paul and Thecla*, 45.

anything but tear off bits of her garment and, with the confirmation of the material in their hands, embrace faith.

Unlike Thecla, Emmelia had neither father nor betrothed to object to her wish to live as a virgin, but this did not mean her way was clear. Without the protection of a male guardian, a woman's situation in the ancient world was quite precarious. In the culture of the ancient Roman Empire the norm for men was an extreme degree of machismo really deserving of the term "toxic masculinity." At that time, it was a fact of life that men might simply abduct women they desired. Some of these abductions were elopements in which women willingly went off with men they wanted to marry—instead of marrying the men their fathers chose. In other cases, however, the women were not at all willing and, once taken in this way, the woman's options were few—she could marry her abductor, if he wanted to marry her, or she could become a beggar, prostitute, or slave.

Around this time, Rome had a new law prohibiting such "bride theft," but this law would not have protected Emmelia. She was not betrothed: abducting her would not constitute bride theft. The law safeguarded the interests and authority of fathers and future husbands; it did not concern itself with the personal safety of women (which was in the hands of their male guardians).

The young Emmelia, living without a male protector on the family estate, was in a vulnerable situation indeed. Nyssen explains:

> Because her body was just springing into full bud and the fame of her fairness had drawn many young men together in pursuit of her hand, there was risk that if she were not by her own choice united with someone, she might against her will suffer some violence because suitors were maddened by her beauty and getting ready to carry her off.[10]

Emmelia wanted one thing more than she wanted the consecrated life, and that was to be wholly guided by the will of God. Her start in life as a fugitive refugee taught her to meet danger and difficulty with prayer. We might imagine her looking at her situation and praying to understand God's will in her life. We do not know how she reached her decision, but eventually she discerned that God was calling her to marriage.

Basil the Elder was among Emmelia's suitors. Ordinarily, marriages were arranged between the fathers of the prospective spouses, while the

---

10. Gregory of Nyssa, *Life of Saint Macrina*, 22.

bride and groom met (perhaps for the first time) at their betrothal. Having no father or male guardian, Emmelia seems to have played a more active role in choosing her husband than was typical in her time, but this also meant that she needed to take every precaution in guarding her reputation as well as her safety. Her marriage arrangements were likely made through an intermediary, perhaps a priest or another respected (male) relative or community member. Basil's mother, Macrina the Elder, as his only living parent, may have been involved in the negotiations as well.

If Emmelia and Basil the Elder met before their betrothal, the meetings would have been brief and chaperoned. It is appealing to imagine the lovely and devout heiress Emmelia strolling through walled gardens with an ardent and articulate Basil, the two young people falling in love as they conversed about their hopes and dreams. There is, however, little basis for imposing such modern romantic fantasies on Emmelia's story. Consistent with the more pragmatic nature of marriage decisions in that time and place, Nyssen tells us simply that Emmelia "chose a man known and proven for the uprightness of his life so that she acquired a guardian for her own life."[11]

Emmelia married, and soon she was preparing for the birth of her first child. As she was about to be, "freed from her labour pain by giving birth to the child, [she] fell asleep . . ."[12] This brief statement is not elaborated, and yet it invites questions. Emmelia was in the throes of hard labor; this was no peaceful nap. Did she lose consciousness? Was she given an herbal remedy to induce sleep? How long had she labored? Did she experience complications? We know that childbirth was much more perilous then—mothers and infants died at rates exponentially higher than today. When Emmelia "fell asleep," she and her baby were very likely in danger.

While she slept, Emmelia had a vision. She found herself holding the baby in her arms. A majestic, greater-than-human form appeared and addressed the baby as "Thecla." After calling the child in this way three times, the glorious being vanished and Emmelia found her labor eased. As she awakened (or came to), the baby was born. Emmelia held the tiny infant in her arms and knew Thecla to be her secret name.

Here we might pause to ask, why was this a *secret* name? Why, after her compelling vision, did Emmelia not openly name the baby Thecla? Nyssen explains it this way: "It seems to me that the apparition spoke that

---

11. Gregory of Nyssa, *Life of Saint Macrina*, 22.
12. Gregory of Nyssa, *Life of Saint Macrina*, 22.

way not so much to guide the mother in the giving of a name, as to foretell the life of the girl and signify by the sharing of the same name the sharing of the same choice of life."[13] In other words, this secret name was the baby's calling; the vocation of holy virginity, which Emmelia had longed for but relinquished, was given instead to her first-born child. And this naming, this blessing and missioning, turned both Emmelia and her baby back from death's door, brought them back to life.

Nyssen also alludes to another reason that Thecla might have been a secret name—the prevailing cultural tradition of honoring family members in the names of children. "Some time ago, there had been a celebrated Macrina in our family . . . At the time of the persecutions she had suffered bravely for her confession of faith in Christ, and it was in honour of her that the child was given [the name Macrina] by her parents."[14] Basil the Elder's oldest daughter really could only be named for his mother Macrina—anything else would have been strange, if not frankly offensive.

This brings us to another interesting question: where was Basil the Elder in all of this? There is no record of his response to his wife's childbed vision, but we know that he absolutely expected Macrina to marry when she came of age. As we will see in the next chapters, there is no sign that father Basil in any way anticipated her calling, nor did he embrace it when she gave it voice. Perhaps Emmelia, and the other women who attended the birth (almost certainly including grandmother Macrina), kept the vision and the name a secret from *him*. If so, why? On the other hand, did Basil know about the vision and the secret name and reject them?

Whatever the case, in Nyssen's narrative, Macrina's birth story serves to show that her calling came from an authentic and holy source: the calling comes to her mother just at the moment when Emmelia has spent all her resources in the effort to bring Macrina into the world. The spiritual force of the calling eases Emmelia's labor and carries mother and child back from the verge of death, back into life. Macrina is given her calling/secret name by a spiritual being, one who knows things beyond human comprehension. She is called before she is born—clearly her personal will is not at work. Occurring in secret, Macrina's calling/naming is an event within the spiritual "inner room," between her soul and God. This is no vanity show; it is not influenced one way or another by the views of other people. From the birth story we know that hers was a pure, true, intrinsic

---

13. Gregory of Nyssa, *Life of Macrina* (trans. Silvas), 112.
14. Gregory of Nyssa, *Life of Saint Macrina* (trans. Corrigan), 22.

calling, like the words of Jer 1:5: "Before I formed you in the womb, I knew you, and before you were born, I consecrated you."

In this chapter, we have seen three women who experienced callings from God. Each of their callings came in a different form. Thecla, who had been contracted in marriage by her father, found herself called to a life of holy chastity, ministry, and healing through the inspiring instruction of the apostle Paul. Emmelia, who wanted to be called to the life of the virgin philosopher, heard God calling through the events of her life, leading her instead to marry. The baby Macrina was first called in a vision given to her mother; her calling was her secret name.

Meditation

The lives of saints turn on the experience of calling—the point at which the person's focus shifts from other goals and concerns to center on holy vocation. Monks, sisters, and clergy often enter the religious life in response to some form of experienced-calling, but calling is not only for saints, vowed religious, and clergy: each us are called.

Consider calling in your life. Some people have dreams, visions, or powerful prayer experiences, but calling can come in other ways as well. Have you found yourself called to work, service, activism, personal commitments, or creative expression through the experiences of your life? Through an inspiring teacher? Through a deep and compelling drive rising within your being? If you had a secret name what would it be?

Consider these passages: John 10:2–5, Ps 139 1–16, 1 Cor 12:4–13, 27–28, or 1 Cor 7:21–24. As in the previous chapters, choose a passage and read it once to know what the words say. Read it a second time to feel how the words resound within you. Read it a third time and rest in quiet, prayerful readiness for any door the Word may open to you.

4

Wisdom, Wool, and Womanhood

"The beginning of wisdom is the most sincere desire for instruction, and concern for instruction is love of [wisdom]." (Wis 6:17)

BABY MACRINA WAS ASSIGNED a servant nurse, as was customary in aristocratic families, but Emmelia chose to nurse her first child personally. Carrier of a secret name and, through that name, of the vocation her mother had surrendered, Macrina was nourished from her mother's body, fed and formed through her mother's work and wisdom. Grandmother Macrina the Elder, all the while, guided and watched over mother and child.

Emmelia was thoughtful and deliberate in designing young Macrina's education. She rejected the customary curriculum of the day, which started children out on classic pagan literature such as the Homeric epics and Greek plays. Nyssen tells us that Emmelia found these materials "disgraceful and altogether unsuitable to teach a tender and impressionable nature either the tragic passions—those passions of women which gave the poets their starting points and themes, or the indecencies of comedy, or the causes of the miseries that befell Troy, which through their degrading tales concerning women tend to the corruption of character."[1]

Before dismissing Emmelia as narrow-minded and censorious, it may be worth taking a closer look at the materials in question. Among the most well-known and widely-read was Homer's great epic poem *The Iliad* (set during the Trojan War). This narrative begins with the (married) Greek

---

1. Gregory of Nyssa, *Life of Macrina* (trans. Silvas), 113.

king Agamemnon and heroic warrior Achilles claiming beautiful women (one of them the wife of an important man in Troy) as battle prizes—that is, taking these women as slaves to satisfy their lust. Agamemnon then demands Achilles's sex slave for himself, and Achilles unhappily gives her over but goes into a spiteful and vengeful rage and refuses to fight for king and country. The Greek army is soon in peril of defeat, one of their ships is burned and many warriors are wounded. Achilles, although still bent on teaching Agamemnon a lesson and getting his sex slave back, does not want the Trojan army to burn his own ships. Wrapped up in pride, rage, lust, and self-interest, Achilles sends his closest friend Patroclus into battle wearing his (Achilles's) armor. The idea was that this would so frighten the Trojans that the Greeks would prevail even without the benefit of Achilles's actual battle prowess. The ploy works until the gods get involved.

Acting on motives of favoritism, power struggles amongst themselves, or capricious whims, the gods intervene in various ways, with the result that Patroclus is killed by a great Trojan warrior named Hector. Filled with grief and even more rage, Achilles does not forgive Agamemnon but makes a strategic decision to join forces with him in avenging the death of his friend. There follows a bloodbath. Eventually Achilles kills Hector. In a series of utterly ghastly scenes, Achilles denigrates Hector's remains by tying the body to the back of his chariot and dragging it across the battlefield, then dragging it in circles around Patroclus's funeral bier. Hector's father is reduced to begging for the body of his son.

Like *The Iliad*, other classical literature read widely in Emmelia's day also features characters and gods who are motivated by impulses of anger, pride, lust, jealousy, greed, favoritism, self-interest, and revenge. Common plot elements include scheming, dishonesty, theft, rape, dishonoring of parents, adultery, suicide, murder, and war atrocities. Many people today might share Emmelia's view that, however worthwhile for older readers, these are not the ideal materials to use in the education of young children.

Emmelia's sources on education included Plato. In his *Republic* (written around 375 BCE), Plato (in the voice of Socrates) takes up the education of children. He argues that society needs people who are spirited and also gentle, who can be fierce guardians and protectors, and who also love wisdom. He makes the case that, to shape people of such character, society must carefully choose what children hear and learn; in particular, Socrates asserts, children should never be exposed to the stories of Homer, Hesiod, and the other ancient poets, in which Gods and heroes freely engage in utmost wrong. These works are composed of "false stories" that portray the gods in a way that bears no resemblance to true divine nature: unlike the fickle, flawed, and self-interested deities in the ancient pagan stories, he says, in truth God is *good*. God *is* good. Entirely and only good, God causes good and good only.

Socrates allows that the works of the ancient poets, even while presenting a false picture of the divine, hold rich allegorical lessons. However, he points out that the young do not understand the difference between allegory and accurate depiction, and thus, he says, these works are entirely unsuitable for young persons[2] (see Appendix 1).

Emmelia's view of classical Greek literature may have been influenced by these arguments, or perhaps she found in Plato an authority who agreed with her own independent response to these works. In any case, she chose to educate the young Macrina from Holy Scripture rather than Greek poetry and drama, and from Holy Scripture she chose especially the Wisdom of Solomon, Proverbs, and the Psalter.

As we saw in chapter 2, Origen quoted the Wisdom of Solomon in explaining the true purpose of human life. Nyssen's treatise *On Virginity* also draws from the teachings of this biblical book. Although part of the present-day Roman Catholic and Eastern Orthodox canons, the Wisdom of Solomon is a book of the Bible unknown to many Protestants. It is considered apocryphal by most Protestant sects and so usually omitted from Protestant Bibles, except those editions designated as "including the Apocrypha." The book is a work in praise and celebration of wisdom and an exhortation to live, and guide for living, a life of practiced wisdom—a life of justice and virtue. The book of Wisdom was at the core of Emmelia's approach to teaching and formation. Indeed, she embodied the "concern for instruction" that is called the love of wisdom in our opening quote, and she instilled in her children that "most sincere desire for instruction" from which wisdom grows.

There is another feature of the book of Wisdom that may have been significant for Emmelia and Macrina: throughout the book, wisdom is assigned feminine pronouns.

> There is in her a spirit that is intelligent, holy, unique, manifest, subtle, mobile, clear, unpolluted, distinct invulnerable, loving the good, keen, irresistible, beneficent, humane, steadfast, sure, free from anxiety, all powerful, overseeing all, and penetrating through

---

2. Plato, *Republic*, Book II, 377–82.

> all spirits ... For wisdom is more mobile than any motion; because of her pureness she pervades and penetrates all things. For she is a breath of the power of God and a pure emanation of the glory of the Almighty. (Wis 7:22–25)

> Although she is but one, she can do all things, and while remaining in herself, she renews all things; in every generation she passes into holy souls and makes them friends of God, and prophets; for God loves nothing so much as the person who lives with Wisdom. She is more beautiful than the sun, and excels every constellation of the stars. (Wis 7:27–29)

Unlike many ancient writings in which the female is depicted as inferior, weak, evil, malevolently seductive, or shamed and corrupted by lascivious attentions, this book describes wisdom as desirable and beautiful in being intelligent, virtuous, supremely competent, and thoroughly worthy. Here the teacher, leader, way to redemption, is called she/her, bride, and mother:

> I loved her and sought her from my youth; I desired to take her for my bride, and became enamored of her beauty ... She knows the things of old, and infers the things to come; she understands turns of speech and the solutions of riddles; she has foreknowledge of signs and wonders and of the outcomes of seasons and times. Therefore I determined to take her to live with me, knowing that she would give me good counsel and encouragement in cares and grief. (Wis 8:2; 8–9)

> I loved her more than health and beauty, and I chose to have her rather than light, because her radiance never ceases. All good things came to me along with her, and in her hands uncounted wealth. I rejoiced in them all, because wisdom leads them; but I did not know that she was their mother. (Wis 7:10–12)

The Wisdom of Solomon, then, provided Emmelia's little girl with instruction on how to live the faith while also teaching her that value, spiritual good, and likeness to God can exist in feminine form. In applied practice of these lessons, little Macrina's days were patterned on the rhythm of prayer passed down from Thaumaturgus by her refugee parents and grandparents. Nyssen tells us:

> There was nothing whatever of the Psalter that she did not know, since she recited each part of the psalmody at its own proper time. When she rose from bed, or began her duties or rested from them,

or sat down to eat or retired from table, when she went to bed or rose for prayers, she kept up the psalmody wherever she went, like a good travelling companion that never left her at any time.[3]

Macrina's duties very likely included lessons, feminine domestic tasks, and helping with her younger siblings. In her growing family, there was always a new baby to take up the time and energy of her mother and the nurses who cared for the younger children. By the time Macrina was four, her brother Basil was two and Naucratius an infant. Gregory was born when she was seven, there was a baby boy that did not survive, and she also had four little sisters whose birthdates are not recorded. Her youngest brother Peter was born when she was eighteen.

Summing up Macrina's early years in one of his wonderful, meaningpacked-yet-unelaborated remarks Nyssen says: "having become especially skilled in the working of wool, she attained her twelfth year."[4] To unpack this brief comment, twelve was not just another birthday—under Roman law, this was the day when a girl became a marriageable woman. Neither was wool-working an incidental hobby. In the modern West we do not really have a frame of reference that lends itself to understanding the significance of wool skills for a girl in Macrina's society and so, to open a door into her world, a brief sketch of wool history and customs—a bit of wool gathering as it were—may be of use.

The culture of wool-working in Macrina's time was an inheritance woven over thousands of years, rooted in the relationship between human communities and the wild sheep whose meat and hides fed and clothed neolithic tribes in Asia Minor for untold centuries, 12,000 years ago and more. Uses of sheep's fur twisted into string evolved into the invention of woolen textiles. Over time, the animals were domesticated and selected for woolier coats while tools and traditions developed around keeping sheep, processing wool, and weaving cloth.

Wool production was a resource-intensive enterprise that involved the entire community. In the ancient division of labor, men were the warriors who won and held the territory necessary to graze flocks, the shepherds who tended, fed, and guarded the sheep, and the merchants who traded the finished products. Meanwhile, the labor, craft, and traditions of wool-working were the domains of women.[5] Women hand-plucked and combed

3. Gregory of Nyssa, *Life of Macrina* (trans. Silvas), 113–14.
4. Gregory of Nyssa, *Life of Saint Macrina* (trans. Corrigan), 23.
5. Thomasson, "Her Share," 93–112.

hair from the earliest types of sheep (see Appendix 1). Whether wool was plucked or sheared, women processed the raw fiber—they washed, sorted, combed, spun, dyed, wove, and sewed.

Until around 2000–2500 BCE, wool-working was a home-based activity. Women in extended family households processed and wove wool in between and alongside their other tasks, such as gardening, cleaning, food preparation, and childcare.[6] The work, especially in the production of finer fabrics, was slow and labor intensive, and while working at home, these women were not only supplying family and community need: they were making cloth to be sold in a busy and growing trade economy. One window onto the pressures experienced by these early cottage-industry workers is found in a letter written in the second millennium BCE by an Assyrian woman, Lamassi, to her husband who was in Anatolia selling cloth. The letter is found on a cuneiform tablet excavated at the ancient city of Karum Kanesh in east-central Anatolia, at modern Kultepe. Lamassi writes:

> Kulumaya is bringing you nine textiles. Iddin-Sin is bringing you three textiles . . . Please my master, don't get angry because I haven't sent you the textiles you asked for in your letter. Oh, how the little one has grown and I had to make a couple of thick blankets for the cart. You see, I've only been making things for the house and the family, that's why I haven't sent you any textiles [to sell]. Ok, I'll send all of the textiles that I can produce on the next caravan . . .[7]

Another passage about textile production and the busy lives of ancient women is one that Macrina would have known well, found in Proverbs 31:10–27:

> A capable wife who can find? She is far more precious than jewels. The heart of her husband trusts in her, and he will have no lack of gain. She does him good, and not harm, all the days of her life. She seeks wool and flax, and works with willing hands. She is like the ships of the merchant, she brings food from far away. She rises while it is still night and provides food for her household and tasks for her servant girls. She considers a field and buys it; with the fruit of her hands she plants a vineyard. She girds herself with strength, and makes her arms strong. She perceives that her merchandise is profitable. Her lamp does not go out at night. She puts her hand to the distaff, and her hands hold the spindle. She opens her hand to the poor, and reaches her hands to the needy.

6. Lumb, "Textiles, Value, and Early Economies," 54–77.
7. Thomason, "Her Share," 93.

She is not afraid for her household when it snows, for all her household are clothed in crimson. She makes herself coverings; her clothing is fine linen and purple. Her husband is known in the city gates, taking his seat among the elders of the land. She makes linen garments and sells them, she supplies the merchant with sashes. Strength and dignity are her clothing, and she laughs at the time to come. She opens her mouth with wisdom, and the teaching of kindness is on her tongue. She looks well to the ways of her household and does not eat the bread of idleness.

As trade in the region grew in scale, wool actually became so important and so valuable that, in the pre-monetary economy of the early bronze age, it came to serve all the purposes of a currency.[8] Workers were paid in wool, wool was saved and traded internationally, units of wool were exchanged for goods. In a word, wool was as good as gold—perhaps casting new light on the (later European) fairy tale of Rumpelstiltskin and the girl who was tasked with spinning straw into gold!

Given the value of wool, it is not surprising that Mesopotamian societies raced to expand their wool production capacities. This led to the first organized, controlled supply chains and the first urban, industrial workshops in human history. Thousands of women and children (as well as some men) worked in urban textile plants processing wool—spinning and weaving it into the gold of their economy. Meanwhile, throughout the Near East, women in villages and on farms and estates continued the tradition and culture of wool-working at home.

Beyond their economic significance, wool and wool-working also carried cultural and religious meaning for the people of the ancient Near East. Wool is often referenced as a symbol of purity and cleanness in ancient texts, including Hebrew Scripture. Wool and wool craft are discussed as important aspects of, and evidence of, God's foresight and beneficence. Macrina's brother Basil put it this way: "Each of the arts is God's gift to us, remedying the deficiencies of our natures, as, for example . . . the art of weaving, since the use of clothing is necessary for decency's sake and for protection against the wind . . ."[9] Similarly, Nyssen saw evidence of God's plan for a human role in tending creation as evidenced by the correspondence between animal gifts and human needs. He pointed out that humans lack features that are common in animals and could be very helpful in our lives: "Man

---

8. Breniquet, "Wool Economy," 14–35.
9. Basil of Caesarea, *Complete Works, Long Rules 55*, Loc 15854.

is brought to life bare of natural covering, . . . a poor being, destitute of all things useful . . . not armed with prominent horns or sharp claws, nor with hoofs nor with teeth, nor possessing by nature any deadly venom in a sting . . ."[10] Our unimpressive and inadequate equipment, he suggests, is part of God's grand design because it provides the basis for our relationships with animals and gives us a reason to do our work in tending creation:

> If man had such power as to be able to outrun the horse . . . and to carry upon him horns and stings and claws, he would be, to begin with, a wild-looking and formidable creature . . . and moreover he would have neglected his [role in tending] the other creatures if he had no need of [their] co-operation . . . It was the slowness and difficult motion of our body that brought the horse to supply our need, and tamed him; it was the nakedness of our body that made necessary our management of sheep, which supplies the deficiency of our nature by its yearly produce of wool . . .[11]

Textile-working was also seen as evidence and expression of intelligence and beyond this, of wisdom and creative potency. Macrina's family-friend and contemporary, St. Gregory of Nazianzus (Nazianzen), considers what their textile skills might say about women: "Holy scripture admires the cleverness in weaving even of women, saying, Who gave to woman skill in weaving and cleverness in the art of embroidery? This belongeth to a living creature that hath reason, and exceedeth in wisdom and maketh way even as far as the things of heaven."[12] In Exodus 35:25–27 we read of the Israelites preparing a great tribute to God (here quoting Robert Alter's translation): "Every woman wise-hearted with her hands spun and brought threadwork of indigo and purple and crimson linen. And all the women whose hearts moved them with wisdom spun the goat hair." Proverbs 31:20 tells us that the woman whose hands work the distaff and spindle (see Appendix 1) by lamplight can also open her hand to the poor and reach out to the needy. Further, "She opens her mouth with wisdom, and the teaching of kindness is on her tongue" (Prov 31:26).

Basil speaks of weaving, among other arts, as a simile for God's acts of creation: "such are the arts which work in wood and brass and weaving . . . [that], even when the artisan has disappeared, serve to show an industrious

---

10. Gregory of Nyssa, *Collection, On the Making of Man VII:1*, Loc 10941.

11. Gregory of Nyssa, *Collection, On the Making of Man VII:2*, Loc 10953.

12. Gregory of Nazianzus, *Collection, Oration XXVII: The Second Theological Oration*, Loc 4772.

intelligence and to cause the [builder, smith, or] weaver, to be admired . . . [Likewise] the world is a work of art displayed for the beholding of all people; to make them know Him who created it."[13] Basil is saying that creation is a work of art through which we can know God.

As told by Nyssen, Macrina herself later picks up this analogy in a dialectic about faith: "Anyone who sees a garment will reason to the weaver . . . But small souls gaze upon the world and their eyes are blind to the one who is declared through all these things."[14]

The art and craft of wool-working were woven into female culture and traditions in Macrina's world. Skill in wool-working was associated with value and status among women, for whom abilities in this area might open opportunities and distinguish and enrich family members. Girls who could produce fine woolens were prized in the marriage market. Proverbs 31:23 tells us that the husband of the woman who spins through the night "is known in the city gates, taking his seat among the elders of the land."

As a little girl, Macrina likely learned to sort and comb wool and then to spin using a drop spindle. This is by no means an easy task for a child—to produce a tight, strong, and even thread, the spinner must keep the loose wool at the ready but free from tangles and at the same time hold the spindle up for extended periods while controlling tension and motion. Likewise, weaving involved long hours at a loom, perhaps a vertical loom or a warp-weighted loom, with mother, grandmother, or other women of the household working alongside or instructing and guiding her labors. The young Macrina would have needed uncommon focus, patience, and diligence to develop journeyman level wool-working skills at age twelve. As she crossed the threshold from childhood to marriageable age, she was showing every sign of wisdom and virtue, every promise of becoming the capable wife described in Proverbs 31.

Meditation

Wisdom is the applied form of knowing. To be wise is to have clear and accurate knowledge of what is real, what is true, what is good, and to integrate this fully in what we do.

Wisdom is being the good we want to see, as the slogan goes. It is divine action channeled through human hands, the work of God carried

---

13. Basil of Caesarea, *Hexaemeron*, Homily I:7, Loc 3682.
14. Gregory of Nyssa, *On the Soul and Resurrection* (trans. Silvas), 175.

out on human scale; it is engaging all our knowledge, time, and abilities to do what is loving, just, merciful, and needful.

Macrina's early life is the story of a mother, a grandmother, and a growing child seeking to live out wisdom. They gave and received instruction in both philosophy and the practical skills to do the needful, merciful, and just, from learning the Psalter by heart to the art and craft of wool-working. In their study of the Word, in their work as producers of textiles for their community and for trade, in their prayer and psalmody through the hours of their days, they sought to make wisdom the basis of their choices and their actions.

Have you known people who seemed to live the life of wisdom as Macrina and her mother and grandmother sought to do? Who were they and how have the affected your life?

Where or how do you find wisdom now?

How does wisdom guide your daily activities? Are there things you feel drawn to do, or stop doing, to bring your daily life into closer alignment with wisdom?

Consider the following passages or others, choose a passage that speaks to you, and read it three times as we have done before, first with attention to what the words say, second with attention to what they stir in you, and finally with prayerful awareness of any doors that may be opened: Luke 2:40, Luke 7:35, Matt 7:15–20, or Wis 6:17–20, 7:15–24, 7:25–30, 8:21.

5

Vocation

"Lead the life that the Lord has assigned, to which God called you." (1 Cor 7:17)

ON HER TWELFTH BIRTHDAY, Macrina was of marriageable age under Roman law, and she had everything that could be desired in a bride. She was a devout and virtuous girl and an especially skilled wool-worker. As the eldest daughter of a well-to-do and influential family, she would bring a future husband a large dowry and advantageous business connections. She was even a great beauty. Her brother Nyssen comments that despite her modesty, her attractions became known: "It is indeed worth marveling how the beauty of the young girl, although concealed, did not remain unnoticed. There did not seem to be any such marvel in the whole of that country which could compare with her beauty and gracefulness, so that not even painters' hands could come close to her fresh beauty."[1] As a result, much like her mother as a young woman, Macrina was beset by "a great swarm" of suitors.

Her father decided to settle matters by betrothing her to a man who was of similar social standing with upright character, family connections, and excellent prospects. The chosen man had just completed studies in rhetoric (something like modern law school) and was perhaps twenty years old.

But wait, we are thinking, this is the girl with the secret name, the calling to become a virgin philosopher! How can she abandon her true identity,

---

1. Gregory of Nyssa, *Life of Saint Macrina* (trans. Corrigan), 24.

Thecla, to be married? Nyssen's narrative implies that Macrina faced a conflict between filial obedience and inward call. He tells us that Macrina was "not ignorant"[2] of her father's plans, but he does not go into her thoughts and feelings. As we have seen, by custom and by law, marriages were decided and arranged by fathers—the opinions of daughters and their mothers had no legal standing, but human relationships would surely have made the wishes of women relevant to many fathers. In this family's story Elder Basil's decision is certainly puzzling. Whatever his reasoning, however, his decision was made and Macrina could not legally refuse to marry the man her father chose unless she could show him to be unworthy in terms of social standing or moral behavior, which he was not.

Once the marriage was arranged, it was the tradition that the young people met (often for the first time) in a formal betrothal ceremony in which the prospective bride and groom consented to the contract of future marriage and exchanged a hand clasp and kiss. There is no indication that this ceremony took place in Macrina's case. Nyssen makes the statement that their father planned to betroth her to the chosen man, "when she came of age," which is somewhat confusing because she was of legally marriageable age at the time. Some historical sources indicate that there may have been a local or Christian custom of betrothal and marriage when girls were a little older, between fifteen and seventeen. Macrina's betrothal was, thus, planned by her father and arranged with the prospective groom and his family but not actually accomplished.

Having never become formally betrothed, Macrina and her intended may not have met. If they did meet, it is unlikely that they knew each other well. They could have been acquainted by face and name from attending the same community events, but girls and young men occupied separate areas at such gatherings, and they were never left alone together.

While he waited for his bride to reach the desired age, the intended groom solidified relations with his future father-in-law and advanced his career. Nyssen tells us that he offered their father "his reputation in eloquence as an especially pleasing kind of wedding gift; for he used to display the power of his eloquence in forensic contests on behalf of the wronged."[3] His prospects were looking very bright in every way for a year or two after the marriage plan was made. Then, suddenly and tragically, he died. As

---

2. Gregory of Nyssa, *Life of Macrina* (trans. Silvas), 115.
3. Gregory of Nyssa, *Life of Macrina* (trans. Silvas), 114.

Nyssen put it, "Envy cut short [his] more purposeful hopes by snatching him away in his pitiful youth."[4]

We do not know the identity of Macrina's young man, but Anna Silvas notes an intriguing coincidence between his story and that of a certain Euphemius, a cousin of close family friend Gregory of Nazianzus.[5] Nazianzen eulogized his cousin saying:

> Euphemius, an orator among orators, a poet among poets, the glory of his country, the glory of his parents, is dead, but just bearded... Alas for the misfortune! Instead of a virgin bride he possesses a tomb, and the day of wailing overtook the days of the bridal song.
>
> Euphemius was a little relic of the golden age, noble alike in character and intellect, gentle, sweet of speech, beautiful as the Graces ... he who was the talk of all Cappadocia, he whom the Graces gave to the Muses. The chanters of the bridal song were at his gate, but Envy came quicker than they.[6]

Not long after his death, suitors crowded around Macrina again, offering her father proposals for her hand. It was at this point that she took a bold and unexpected step: "When the decision which had been made for her was cut off by the young man's death, she designated her father's decision a marriage, as if what had been decided upon had already taken place."[7] When her parents told her of new marriage proposals:

> She would say that it was out of order and unlawful not to be loyal to the marriage that had been authorized once and for all for her by her father and to be put under pressure to consider another; since by nature marriage is but once only, as there is one birth and one death. She insisted that he who had been joined to her by her parents' decision had not died, but that in her judgment he was alive to God through the hope of the resurrection, and was away on a journey, not dead, and that it was out of order not to keep faith with one's bridegroom who had gone abroad.[8]

In this way, Macrina construed her father's decision about her future marriage as having all the weight and finality of a marriage fully

---

4. Gregory of Nyssa, *Life of Macrina* (trans. Silvas), 115.
5. Silvas, *Macrina the Younger*, 115fn29.
6. Henderson, *Greek Anthology Book VIII*, 455–57.
7. Gregory of Nyssa, *Life of Macrina* (trans. Silvas), 115.
8. Gregory of Nyssa, *Life of Macrina* (trans. Silvas), 115–16.

accomplished. Her response may have seemed a bit extreme—a bit dramatic, maybe eccentric. The lives and activities of young men in the ancient world were full of danger, and Macrina would have known of other girls whose intended future husbands perished. Her contemporaries might have considered that for all the sadness of her young man's death, she was better off because he died before they married, leaving her still a fully eligible bride. Macrina's strange insistence that she should be viewed as a widow may have seemed, at first, like nothing more than the hysterics of a young and emotional girl; however, over time the depth of her sincerity and steadfastness of her will proved that it was much more.

In the light of her life afterwards, we see clearly that this was nothing less than her stand for her vocation. But for her it was not a one-and-done step into a cloister or cutting of hair, such as later women monastics used to mark commitment to vocation. Macrina had to defend and reassert her position as the question of marrying her to different men was raised again and again, despite the finality of her argument. Nyssen comments, "Indeed her decision was more firmly fixed than might have been expected at her age."[9]

Her position was precarious, easily challenged, at odds with the expectations and customs of the society around her, and subject to override by her father. Still, on the thin pretext of assumed widowhood, this thirteen- or fourteen-year-old girl stood firm in asserting her calling—her intention to remain unmarried and devote herself to the pursuit of philosophy (i.e., vowed virginity and dedication to wisdom lived). She turned obedience to her father into a shield against the pressure to marry, claimed the vocation her mother had to give up, and did so without incurring the terrible consequences Thecla faced.

Was her self-designation as widow an ingenious maneuver, or was it a simple and sincere response to her situation? Convincing arguments can be made both ways (see Appendix 1), and possibly Macrina's response reflected both grief over the death of the young man to whom she was promised *and* an affirmed and amplified experience of calling.

The youthful Macrina undoubtedly showed remarkable courage, ingenuity, and determination in taking her stand. For all her bravery and cleverness, however, there is no indication that her father ever accepted her decision, and he could, at any point, have chosen to overrule her objections and compel her to marry. For the next four or five years, Macrina seems to have practiced her vocation privately through a life of prayer and devoted

---

9. Gregory of Nyssa, *Life of Macrina* (trans. Silvas), 115.

service within her family. She helped her mother, educated the younger children, and sustained a quiet but unwavering resistance to the marriage agenda. Her father tried to persuade her to accept marriage proposals, perhaps testing her determination, but stopped short of forcing her hand. Very likely, many fathers in that time and place would have been less patient. We are left to wonder what Elder Basil thought and planned. Was he considering the idea of endorsing her vocation? Was he biding his time, planning to press the issue when he found an especially advantageous match, or when she had more time to recover from the loss of her intended? Was Elder Basil himself unsure what to do and seeking a sign, a sense of direction from God? Alternatively, was he so busy and distracted with other things that he did not have time to focus on this matter?

Certainly, Elder Basil had many things to occupy his mind, not least of which were literal and figurative tectonic shifts in the country where they lived. Soon after assuming power, Emperor Constantine (who had declared Christianity the imperial religion) made a radical move: he decided to leave Rome, the Eternal City, ancient and celebrated birthplace of the empire, and establish a new capital. For his new city, he chose the site of ancient Byzantium, about 450 miles west of Pontus at the Bosporus Strait (which joins the Black Sea to the Marmara Sea). The city was to be nothing less than a "second Rome," with all the grandeur, culture, size, and amenities of Rome herself.

This massive project called for supplies of every kind. A great road was built all the way from Antioch (on the Mediterranean coast) through Cappadocia to bring materials from the region to the new city—a road that skirted, and perhaps in places passed through, Elder Basil's landholdings. With the help of this artery, Constantine was said to have stripped the region bare, gathering to his new capital building materials, statues, works of art, textiles, historical artifacts, and religious relics, as well as laborers and supplies of grain, meat, and clothing.

Just six years after becoming sole emperor, when Macrina was three years old, Constantine inaugurated his new capital Constantinople (modern Istanbul). The city continued to grow in the following years, and the Imperial Senate, courts, and administration drew elites from all over the empire. These people expected to be supplied with servants, fine food and clothing, and luxurious living arrangements. Their demands placed constant economic pressure on the surrounding countryside.

The people most immediately feeling that pressure were local aristocrats, native to the region, who were required to deliver tax payments to the governors of their provinces. These taxes were levied in many forms—not just money but foodstuffs, laborers, livestock, metal ore, wool fiber, textiles, and clothing. Land-owning men, like Basil the Elder, traditionally used the produce of their estates to sustain their own aristocratic lifestyle and maintain their workforce of slaves and peasant laborers. The empire now demanded a good share of that produce, and the local landowners found themselves squeezed from both directions.

When Macrina was ten (337), Constantine died and left the rule of the empire divided between his two sons; the western regions ruled from Rome and the eastern from Constantinople. The new emperor of the East, Constantinius II, was a tough, hard-driving man who was faced with unrest on multiple frontiers. To put down challenges to the empire, he needed armies and all the resources to equip, sustain, and command them. To raise and sustain armies, he needed not only soldiers but influencers, administrators, and producers of goods. He and his governors looked to fill these needs by offering the local aristocracy opportunities in the imperial administration. If they signed on, these locals might anticipate various appealing rewards. They would be able to address higher officials with requests on behalf of the people in their communities, even appeal directly to the emperor if they chose, and being in such positions of influence would make them sought-after and important. With the promise of both imperial privilege and increased local prominence and reputation, aligning with the empire was tempting. At the same time, however, taking such a position meant dividing their loyalties—they would be working for an emperor whose business was occupying their land and exploiting their own resources.

Basil the Elder was just the sort of local notable that Constantinius's administration would have wanted to enlist. A lawyer and teacher of rhetoric, a landed aristocrat with estates in three provinces, and a prominent citizen of his region, he would have felt the pressures of both imperial recruiting and local concern for autonomy and justice. Managing his large and widespread holdings, running a school for aristocratic boys (including his own sons), looking out for family interests, staying apprised of rapidly changing alliances around him, and participating in local and regional developments surely made him a very busy man.

Adding to Elder Basil's stress, his mother, Macrina the Elder, died in 340, around the same time as young Macrina's intended groom. Also around this time, possibly in 344 (the year Macrina turned seventeen), there was a major earthquake that leveled Basil's home city of Neocaesaria. The only building left standing was the cathedral built by Thaumaturgus. That same year, Emmelia became pregnant with their tenth child (counting the son who died in infancy) at what was then a rather advanced age for childbearing (between thirty-five and thirty-nine).

With all of this on his mind, his unusual eldest daughter and her peculiar resistance to marriage may not have been Elder Basil's greatest concern. Indeed, the enormous pressures he faced were likely taking a great toll on him. Around age forty-nine, before his last child was born, he died. His death was not violent and there is no mention of an illness or injury. There were no preparations, and there is no record of last words. Whatever happened was swift and unexpected—like someone taken by a heart attack.

Besides his pregnant widow, Basil the Elder left Macrina aged eighteen, Basil Jr. sixteen, Naucratius fourteen, Gregory (Nyssen) ten, and Macrina's four little sisters whose ages may have been anywhere between two and twelve.

Meditation

Read the following passages, or others of your choosing, three times as before: first to know what they say, then to listen to your own response, and then to see what the Spirit might open to you. Luke 1:4–45, Mark 6:1–6, 1 Cor 7:20–24.

Vocation is the work that expresses one's true calling, the work of the soul. How is your sense of calling met in your life? When and where do you feel closest to doing exactly what you were made and meant to do? If you could do anything, what would you do?

6

The Bread of Life

"The kingdom of heaven is like yeast that a woman took and mixed in with three measures of flour, until all of it was leavened." (Matt 13:33)

THROUGH HER TEENS, WHEN other girls were marrying and starting families, Macrina quietly pursued her calling as a virgin philosopher within her father's house, apparently without any formal sanction or recognition. With his death, she and Emmelia found themselves in a position of new autonomy: under Roman law, widowhood was the one situation in which a woman was a free person, subject to neither father nor husband. This allowed Macrina to step into a more active leadership role in her family, and as she did so, her practice of vocation activated profound change in her household and everyone around her. Gradually over the decades to come, Macrina's lived philosophy would so permeate and inspire the whole community that, gradually and by stages, the aristocratic estate was transformed to a monastery.

Central to Macrina's philosophy was *theosis*—that idea briefly touched upon in chapter 2 when we saw how Origen melded Greek philosophy with Christian mysticism. Macrina's idea of theosis was based in her understanding of how the human is created in the likeness of God, drawn from her own study of Scripture, and influenced by Origen's teachings.

Macrina was raised on the Wisdom of Solomon, the same biblical book that Origen quoted in explaining his philosophy of faith. The words quoted by Origen are especially germane in understanding her outlook:

"[Wisdom] is a breath of the power of God, and pure emanation of the glory of the Almighty. For she is a reflection of eternal light, a spotless mirror of the working of God, and an image of his goodness" (Wisdom 7:25a, 26). Macrina used this metaphor, the mirror, in explaining her philosophy of theosis. While we will never be the same as God, she taught, we are created in God's image as a reflection is created in a glass:

> Often in a small fragment of glass, when it happens to lie in the sunlight, the whole circle of the sun is seen, not appearing in it according to its own size, but as the smallness of the fragment allows the reflection of the sun's circle. In the same way the smallness of our nature reflects the image of those ineffable properties of divinity.[1]

In chapter 4, we visited the beautiful idea, discussed by Basil and Nyssen, that creation can be considered as a work of art through which we encounter the activity and being of the artist, God. The idea of theosis develops our understanding of our journey as created beings still further. When we think of ourselves as artworks, as God's small self-portraits sculpted in mud, our creator's work seems already done, and our creator a distant figure watching us from afar. Understanding ourselves as created in God's likeness through the imaging of God in the mirror of our souls has profoundly different implications. When considered in this way, being made in the image of God no longer appears as an act already done but as something happening here and now, a live-action, real-time, immediate, dynamic relationship of becoming (see Appendix 1).

Theosis is a relationship with a God who is fully present, actively presenting Godness to a soul that has the potential and the possibility to hold, even if in miniature, the fullness of the divine. The fidelity, clarity, and extent to which the likeness of God is created in our soul depends on the state of the mirror: whether the glass is clean or tarnished, warped or true, which way we turn, and whether we "lie in the light." Turning away from God leaves us in the darkness, to be created in the image of things other than God. Turning part way toward God, while bending surreptitiously toward self-interest, warps the mirror and distorts the likeness of God that we are able to reflect. Greed and self-serving attachments tarnish and crust the mirror. Sin can shatter the living reflection of God. By turning toward God, by releasing whatever blocks the light, we can grow ever more able to be created in the image.

1. Gregory of Nyssa, *On the Soul and the Resurrection* (trans. Roth), 45.

Macrina dedicated her life to developing and putting into to action, in her own way, the idea Origen articulated when he said, "The highest good, then, after which the whole of rational nature is seeking, which is called the end of all blessings, is defined by many philosophers as follows: The highest good, they say, is to become as like God as possible."[2] Macrina's life was devoted to theosis—to becoming more able truly and wholly to hold, reveal, and reflect the likeness of God. This was the hope and intention behind everything she did.

As we have seen, Macrina's journey of theosis began even before she was born and became defined when she made her stand for her vocation as a young teen. Her father's death made mother Emmelia a widow which, as we have seen, conferred new autonomy on her. Macrina had claimed the status of widow years before when her young man died, but refusal of marriage seems to have been her only exercise of personal rights during her father's life. Her status under the law would have remained doubtful after his death, but Emmelia's was clear. As a widow, she had the authority to make choices about herself and her family, she could own property in all forms, and she could transact business (or at least authorize its transaction by male representatives). By both naming herself a widow and working within the shelter of her mother's legal authority, Marcrina was able to function as active hub and leader of her family.

At the same time that widowhood freed women, however, it also brought its own hardships. Widows faced not only the grief of bereavement but sometimes-onerous mourning conventions, lowered social status, and very real practical difficulties. Nyssen, who was old enough at the time of their father's death to understand at least some of what was happening to his mother, sister, and family, later described the experience of the widow in this way:

> [Death] takes off the bridal ornaments and clothes [the bride] in the colors of bereavement. There is darkness in the once cheerful room, and the waiting-women sing their long dirges. She hates her friends when they try to soften her grief; she will not take food, she wastes away, and in her soul's deep dejection has a strong longing only for death . . . Even supposing that time puts an end to this sorrow, still another comes . . . If she has [children], they are fatherless, and, as objects of pity themselves, renew the memory of her loss. If she is childless, then the name of her lost husband is rooted up . . . Some actually take advantage of her affliction. Others exult over

2. Origen, *Complete Works, De Principiis III:6*, 178.

her loss, and see with malignant joy the home falling to pieces, the insolence of servants, and the other distresses visible in such a case ... In consequence of these, many women are compelled to risk once more the trial of the same things [through remarriage], not being able to endure this bitter derision. As if they could revenge insults by increasing their own sufferings![3]

After the death of Elder Basil, Macrina and Emmelia were in a situation of daunting and precarious freedom: Macrina was not legally a widow, and their relative autonomy meant that they had no male guardian to provide protection. The law against bride theft would not protect them, even if it were observed and enforced. They could look only to their servants and the younger children to guard them from any opportunist who might seek to "take advantage of their affliction." At the same time, the two women were suddenly and unexpectedly responsible for management of the extensive and far-spread family estates, for providing for the lives and futures of the eight living younger children, and for carving the path of their own lives ahead in a world where women had very little influence or access. Furthermore, because Basil the Elder had no brothers or other close male relatives, his death left the family without male advocates, mentors, or representatives in his home city of Neocaesaria.

Macrina met these enormous challenges with another unusual, courageous, and extreme decision: she committed herself never to be separated from her mother for even a moment. By staying always with her mother, Macrina made certain that her mother's legal authority would cover everything they did, and she made it impossible for anyone to importune privately upon either of them, protected their reputations and, to some degree at least, guarded their personal safety. Meanwhile, she and her mother decided to leave Neocaesaria and establish a new home at a family estate called Anissa, close to Emmelia's home city of Caesarea in the province of Cappadocia. This allowed Emmelia's male family connections to act as mentors and sponsors for her sons, and to represent her in business dealings that could be conducted only by men.

Annisa was a villa beside the junction of the Iris and Lycus rivers, on the lower slopes of a ridge overlooking a fertile plain and Constantine's great road from Constantinople to Antioch.[4] In the early days at Annisa, Macrina and Emmelia maintained the estate along conventional, aristocratic

---

3. Gregory of Nyssa, *On Virginity*, 16.
4. Silvas, *Macrina the Younger*, 11.

lines (in which the patrician family lived in comfort provided by the labor of servants and slaves) while they supported the younger children and set them on their way in life. Over time, Macrina taught and modeled Gospel life until her household was made over into a monastery where everyone lived simply, aspired to constant worship and prayer, and shared in both labor and its fruits.

Around the year 345, in the beautiful, remote setting of Anissa, the eighteen-year-old Macrina and her bereaved mother committed to being constantly together, never separated for even a moment. To modern ears, this may sound like a dubious plan. How many people of any relation (let alone middle-aged mothers and teen daughters!) could be constantly together without bad temper, resentment, impatience, or simply a need for solitude and privacy? Nyssen also recognizes concerns along these lines as he assures us that Macrina's company was "neither burdensome nor without advantage"[5] for Emmelia. Macrina ministered to her mother's bodily needs, providing services "worth those of many house servants,"[6] and took upon herself the burdens of family and business affairs:

> ... [Macrina] also helped manage all her mother's pressing responsibilities. For she [Emmelia] had four sons and five daughters, and paid taxes to three governors, since her property was scattered in that many provinces.... In all these affairs she shared her mother's toils, dividing the responsibilities with her and lightening the heavy load of her sorrows.[7]

Some authors portray Emmelia as prostrate with grief, and Macrina as ministering to a passive and broken-down mother. Nyssen's narrative does not suggest this—while Macrina tended her mother's bodily needs, he says, Emmelia looked after Macrina's soul. Their closeness was so complete that: "her mother often used to say to her that she had carried her other children in her womb for the appointed time, but that she bore [Macrina] within herself continually, since in a way she sheltered her always in her womb."[8] Thus, "thanks to her mother's guardianship, [Macrina] kept her own life spotless, being directed and witnessed in all things under her mother's eyes, while through her own life she provided a great spur to her mother towards

---

5. Gregory of Nyssa, *Life of Macrina* (trans. Silvas), 116.
6. Gregory of Nyssa, *Life of Macrina* (trans. Silvas), 116.
7. Gregory of Nyssa, *Life of Macrina* (trans. Silvas), 117.
8. Gregory of Nyssa, *Life of Macrina* (trans. Silvas), 116.

... philosophy, little by little drawing her on to the immaterial and unencumbered life."[9]

There was no monastic rule of life for Macrina to follow in her lived faith, no resident virgin philosopher role model to show her the way. She applied herself to labors and practices as she discerned what was fitting to her vocation. Among these, she took upon herself the task of baking bread for communion, "[and] from what was left over she furnished food for her mother from her own labors."[10]

Macrina's bread-baking was an act of deep spiritual and social meaning. In the Gospels and among the first Christians, the breaking of bread referred to a shared meal, and the sharing of meals signified participation in life-in-common, in united work, love, and worship. The first Christian community was knit together in the breaking of bread: "Day by day, as they spent much time together in the temple, they broke bread at home and ate their food with glad and generous hearts, praising God and having the goodwill of all the people" (Acts 2:46). Jesus gave us the breaking and sharing of bread as the enactment of the mystery of faith, the act of embodied union with Christ. "Those who eat my flesh and drink my blood abide in me, and I in them" (John 6:56).

In Macrina's society, bread-making was the job of household slaves. Taking this upon herself was not only an expression of devotion to God and her mother but also an act of humility and a movement toward what we would now call social justice. She was renouncing privilege by doing the work expected of the lowest and least among her household.

Macrina also carried on the rhythms of psalmody, study, work, prayer, and rest that she had learned from her mother and grandmother. Daily communion was an important part of ancient Christian practice.[11] Ordinarily, of course, a priest placed the sacrament of communion onto the tongue of the communicant, but in situations of necessity adaptations were considered acceptable—remote, isolated, and persecuted ancient Christians, who did not have access to church services or priestly visits, could take communion upon their own hands from reserved sacraments.[12] Since there was no priest in the household, Macrina perhaps baked bread to be blessed at a church service or during a visit from a priest, and the household took daily

---

9. Gregory of Nyssa, *Life of Macrina* (trans. Silvas), 116.
10. Gregory of Nyssa, *Life of Macrina* (trans. Silvas), 116.
11. Basil of Caesarea, *Complete Works, Letter Ninety-three*, Loc 7457.
12. Gregory of Nyssa, *Life of Macrina* (trans. Silvas), 116.

communion from the remainder. In this way, while she "lowered" herself by doing the work of slaves, she raised up the people around her, inviting everyone to join in the life of unceasing prayer and full participation in body and being of Christ. Day by day, through her actions, she worked in the leaven that would, in time, transform her household.

In her bread-making, Macrina was fully engaged in the transformative mystery of faith, turning grain into bread, preparing bread to be transformed through the sacrament of communion, in and through communion turning herself from privileged mistress to working companion of people whom her society classed as her possessions, transforming the hierarchical and unequal aristocratic estate into a community of simple, shared, and equal life. She was turning the mirror of her being toward the light by acting in accord with what she discerned as the fullest and truest embodiment of wisdom, all within the context of daily life at home.

Meditation

Read one or more of the following Gospel passages, or others of your choosing, three times. First pay attention to what the words say. Second, pay attention to your thoughts and feelings. Third, hold the Gospel in prayerful awareness and listen for what the spirit may open to you. Mark 14:22–24, John 6:30–35, Mark 6:30–44. Or consider baking bread.

> Simple Wheat Bread
>
> 4 ½ cups bread flour, plus more for kneading
>
> 1 tablespoon sugar
>
> 2 ½ teaspoons salt
>
> 2 teaspoons active dry yeast
>
> 1 2/3 cups lukewarm water

Place the water in a bowl and add the other ingredients except the flour. Mix with a wooden spoon. Add the flour and mix until the ingredients come together into a rough dough. Prepare a clean board with a dusting of flour, turn out the dough and begin to knead: fold the far edge of the dough toward its center, press it down firmly with the heels of your hands, repeat, turn the dough ninety degrees and do the same, and continue to fold and press in a rhythmic, rocking motion for about five or six minutes. The dough should be smooth and springy.

Place the dough in a lightly oiled bowl, cover with a clean tea towel and place in a slightly warm place to rise. Look for the dough to double in size. Depending on the temperature this could take one or two hours.

Deflate the dough and divide in half. Take one of the pieces and pat it into a flattish oval or rectangle. Fold the short ends in as if you are folding a letter, so that the flat dough is folded in thirds, one end in and the other over it. Gently press down the open edge to seal it, and the ends, then gently pat and roll the loaf to elongate it without breaking the skin. When it is about ten inches long, place with sealed fold down on a lightly oiled baking sheet. Repeat with the second loaf.

Cover the loaves and allow to rise about forty-five minutes. Heat oven to 400 degrees. Bake bread twenty minutes or until nicely browned.

7

Hope, Death, and the Ascetic Way

> *"Do not keep striving for what you are to eat and what you are to drink, and do not keep worrying . . . Instead strive for God's kingdom, and these things will be given to you as well . . . Sell your possessions, and give alms. Make purses for yourselves that do not wear out, an unfailing treasure in heaven, where no thief comes near and no moth destroys."*
> *(Luke 12:29, 31, 33)*

MACRINA'S PROGRESS TOWARD A shared gospel life on the family estate took place amidst a wider movement best known through lives and works of the desert fathers and mothers. These ancient ascetic Christians sought to free themselves to live the gospel by renouncing possessions, removing themselves from society, and going to live in remote places. Their experiments in ascetic practice formed the rootstock of the many forms of Christian monasticism.

Desert mothers and fathers were often people of means who chose to renounce their wealth and social status, give all they had to the poor, and dedicate themselves to following the Lord, in literal application of Matt 19:21, where Jesus says to the rich man: "If you wish to be perfect, go, sell your possessions, give the money to the poor, and you will have treasure in heaven; then come, follow me." The desert Christians left their parents and siblings, their homes and communities, their occupations and roles in society and lived in the simplest of huts, as hermits or in groups, practicing extremes of asceticism in the deserts of Egypt, Palestine, Syria, and Arabia. Most of the recorded history of the desert ascetics pertains to men, but women—widows and virgins—were in the desert too. The desert fathers and mothers were, in the words of Metropolitan Anthony Sourozh, "Christians who received the challenge of the Gospel with all earnestness and wanted to respond to it uncompromisingly, as generously as God, with their whole selves."[1]

One of the earliest and most famous of the desert ascetics was the Egyptian Saint Anthony, who lived from about 251 to 356 CE. Macrina was certainly familiar with his life and teaching. His biography was written by his student and long-time attendant, St. Athanasius of Alexandria, who was a contemporary of Basil the Elder. As a young deacon, Athanasius was in Cappadocia, not so far from Macrina's family, to attend the Council of Nicaea (325 CE), where the Nicene Creed was developed. Later, as a bishop, he was a friend and correspondent of Macrina's brother Basil, collaborating with him in defending the faith against the Arian heresy.

Athanasius tells how St. Anthony sought solitude in remote and inaccessible places, and yet many people found him inspiring—so inspiring that would-be monks followed him around, eager to learn from him, and in the process invaded his retreats. Followers hung about outside caves where he tried to withdraw, and at one point, even "began to cast down and wrench off the door by force."[2] These efforts were, perhaps, activated by Anthony's uncommon presence and the hope that contact with him would allow other men to become as he was:

> His soul was free from blemish, for it was neither contracted as if by grief, nor relaxed as by pleasure, nor possessed by laughter or dejection, for he was not troubled when he beheld the crowd [gathered to hear and see him], nor overjoyed at being saluted by so many. But he was altogether even as being guided by reason, and abiding in a natural state.[3]

Anthony was also sought for his power to heal bodily ailments, console the suffering, and bring people in conflict together in the love of Christ. Although generous with his followers, he continued to seek solitude and simplicity. In about 305 CE, he went out to the desert in Egypt. Again, his devotees came after him and, despite his desire to be alone, he responded to their longing and their need. He extended hospitality to these

---

1. Ward, *Sayings of the Desert Fathers*, xv.
2. Athanasius of Alexandria, *Life of St. Anthony of Egypt*, 13.
3. Athanasius of Alexandria, *Life of St. Anthony of Egypt*, 13.

seekers, let them watch and share his practices, and from time to time he spoke with them. They found in him the light of leadership, and around him, in the deserts of Egypt, there grew up the largest wave of the desert ascetic movement: "in the end cells arose even in the mountains, and the desert was colonized by monks who came forth from their own people, and enrolled themselves for the citizenship in the heavens."[4] St. Anthony taught that life should have but one purpose, namely virtue. He said:

> Let us not think, as we look at the world, that we have renounced anything of much consequence, for the whole earth is very small compared with all the heaven . . . Further, we should consider that even if we do not relinquish [worldly possessions] for virtue's sake, still afterwards when we die we shall leave them behind . . . Why not rather get those things which we can take away with us—to wit, prudence, justice, temperance, courage, understanding, love, kindness to the poor, faith in Christ, freedom from wrath, hospitality?[5]

> But to avoid being heedless, it is good to consider the word of the Apostle, I die daily (1 Corinthians 15:31) . . . The meaning of this saying is, that as we rise day by day we should think that we shall not abide till evening; and again when about to lie down to sleep, we should think that we shall not rise up. For our life is uncertain, and Providence allots it to us daily. By thus ordering our life . . . we shall be without wealth, and shall forgive all things to all men, nor shall we retain at all [distracting desires].[6]

In contemporary books and articles, Macrina and her brothers are often included among the desert fathers and mothers. This makes sense in that they lived during the same period, shared the ascetic disposition, and devoted all their efforts to living the gospel. However, when Macrina and her family are lumped together with this larger group, something is lost in understanding what they were doing.

As we saw in chapter 1, central Asia Minor is not the desert. The climate is almost as hot as Egypt in summer and much colder and wetter the rest of the year. Egypt and Cappadocia share average summer high temperatures in the high eighties Fahrenheit, but average winter lows in Egypt are around fifty degrees, while in Cappadocia they are around

---

4. Athanasius of Alexandria, *Life of St. Anthony of Egypt*, 13.
5. Athanasius of Alexandria, *Life of St. Anthony of Egypt*, 14.
6. Athanasius of Alexandria, *Life of St. Anthony of Egypt*, 15.

thirty. Rain is minimal and snow is unknown in the deserts of Egypt; in Cappadocia a month can bring two inches of rain in spring and fall, and eight inches of snow in winter. In Egypt, ascetics could subsist alone in stick huts with one garment, no heat source, rare cooking, and very little food; in Cappadocia life required shelter from the formidable elements, warm clothing, fuel for heat, and food hearty and ample enough to sustain the labors of producing or obtaining these things. Furthermore, the challenging climate and strenuous demands of carving out an existence in the wilds of Asia Minor brought risk of illness and injury. The way of life and regimens of holy discipline practiced by the desert fathers and mothers of milder areas could not easily be recreated in Cappadocia.

Macrina lived not only in a different natural environment but with a vocational calling distinct from that of the desert-dwellers. The desert pilgrims became ascetics by retreating. They gave up position and occupation and placed great barriers of remoteness and inaccessibility between themselves and the demands and distractions of worldly life. Even when they lived in communities in the desert, as some did, they were among fellow retreatants. Macrina did not remove herself—rather, she did what arguably requires even more courage and self-discipline—she transformed herself in place; she stayed put and took upon herself every aspect of worldly life and business. She not only baked bread and did the work of house servants but also became, alongside Emmelia, an executive manager of large and far-flung family estates. She did all of this without becoming distracted from her calling. Rather than leaving society to adopt ascetic practice in isolation, Macrina undertook a home-based, incremental revolution of renunciation and simplicity. She led her community in the practice of poverty, so that at her death, one of the sisters described her possessions:

> There is her cloak, there her head covering, there the worn sandals for her feet. This is her wealth, these are her riches. There is nothing stored up in secret places apart from what you see, or put away safely in chests or bedrooms. She knew of only one place for storing up wealth, the treasure of heaven (Matthew 6:19–20). It was there that she stored her all, leaving nothing behind on earth.[7]

The desert ascetics not only retreated from the business and labor of worldly living, but also left their friends and families behind when they undertook their vocations. In contrast, Macrina remained deeply engaged with her family and the other people in her life. Her ascetic revolution

---

7. Gregory of Nyssa, *Life of Macrina* (trans. Silvas), 138.

was not only domestic but communitarian. She brought along every person willing to join her and tended to each person's progress and struggles with generous attention. By example and practice, over three decades, she brought her household steadily and gently closer and closer to ascetic simplicity, equality, and justice in the details of daily life.

We have seen how Macrina tended her mother with unstinting devotion. Likewise, she brought constant loving presence and careful attention to the care and guidance of her younger brothers and sisters. Among them, the closest to her in age was Basil Jr., the future St. Basil the Great. Macrina was closely involved in supporting his development. The next chapter will explore their relationship in depth. Macrina's second brother, Naucratius, was born when was she was three or four and they grew to share a particular closeness and affinity. According to Nyssen, Naucratius "surpassed the others in good fortune of nature, in beauty of body, in vigor, and in speed and facility in any task."[8] He was gifted with intellectual acuity, mechanical aptitude, athleticism, robust health, and social grace. As the stories in chapter 8 will show, Naucratius's hardiness, good humor, and interpersonal ease were, perhaps, especially appreciated within the family because of their sharp contrast with Basil's frail health and exacting personality.

Little is known about Macrina's four little sisters. One was called Theosebia, but otherwise their names are lost to time. Her third brother, Gregory, Nyssen, was born when she was about eight years old. In a letter written shortly after her death he described her part in his life:

> We had a sister who was for us a teacher of how to live, a mother in place of our mother. Such was her freedom towards God that she was for us a strong tower and a shield of favor as the Scripture says, and a fortified city and a name of utter assurance, through her freedom towards God that came of her way of life.
>
> . . . .she herself imitated the life of angels in a human body. With her there was no distinction between night and day. Rather, the night showed itself active with the deeds of light (Romans 12:12—13; Ephesians 5:8) and day imitated the tranquility of night through serenity of life. The psalmodies resounded in her house at all times through night and day.
>
> You would have seen a reality incredible even to the eyes: the flesh not seeking its own, the stomach, just as we expect in the Resurrection, having finished with its own impulses, streams of tears poured out to the measure of a cup, the mouth meditating

---

8. Gregory of Nyssa, *Life of Macrina*, (trans. Silvas), 118.

the Law at all times, the ear attentive to divine things, the hand ever active... How indeed could one bring before the eyes a reality that transcends description in words?[9]

The youngest brother, Peter, was born after their father's death, when Macrina was about eighteen. He was gifted with aptitude for handcrafts and quickly picked up skills that were usually achieved only through long instruction and practice. Nyssen tells us that Macrina:

> ... took him straight from his nurse and reared him herself. She led him to all the loftier culture, practicing him from infancy in sacred studies, in this way not allowing his soul leisure to incline to any vanity. In this way she became all things to the lad—father, teacher, guardian, mother, counsellor of every good. She so steered him that before he passed the age of boyhood, when he was still in the first bloom of tender youth, he was raised to the lofty goal of philosophy... he preferred before all else to be with his sister and mother, co-working with them towards that angelic life.[10]

Peter's upbringing was a departure from the usual child-rearing practices in ancient Asia Minor, where boys in aristocratic families were instructed at home until reaching school age and then sent out to (male) teachers of Greek grammar and literature. Girls, meanwhile, received their education from the women of their household, remaining in home training until they departed to a husband's household in their teens. Like many of the landed gentry of ancient Asia Minor, father Basil had combined wealth as a landowner with important roles in public debate and in educating the next generation. He was a teacher of Greek grammar and culture. He built such a reputation that families in neighboring regions sent their sons to Neocaesaria to study with him. Nazianzen later wrote that all of Pontus haled Elder Basil as a teacher of virtue.[11] His own sons also attended his school as soon as they were old enough.

In the normal course of things, after this education, around the age of twenty-one, young men were ready to take the next step in their careers. Eldest sons in aristocratic families might be sent away to study in a larger city with the best and most prestigious educators the family could access. They were expected to become heads of the family and leaders in church and society. Younger sons were provided a more pragmatic education and

9. Gregory of Nyssa, *Letter Nineteen*, 87.
10. Gregory of Nyssa, *Life of Macrina*, (trans. Silvas), 122.
11. Van Dam, *Families and Friends in Late Roman Cappadocia*, 18

were expected to become teachers, advocates in the courts, clerks in the imperial bureaucracy, and administrators in family businesses.

Basil, Naucratius, and Nyssen were likely educated by Basil the Elder from their middle childhood until his death when they were about sixteen, fourteen, and ten. After Emmelia and Macrina moved the family to Annisa, the boys studied with teachers in Caesarea. Around age twenty-one, Basil Jr. went on to Constantinople and Athens where he studied under world-renowned teachers. As a second son, Naucratius was not to have the lofty opportunities Basil enjoyed, but even with only a provincial education, his mastery of material and skills in oratory and rhetoric caused something of a sensation. At age twenty-two, (c. 351) he spoke before a full theater (picture here the Roman theaters of the time) and brought down the house. Nyssen does not tell us what he talked about, but Naucratius deeply affected everyone who heard him—people were moved and excited to action by his words. His potential seemed unlimited, and a brilliant career open and ready for his taking. Then, apparently quite suddenly and unexpectedly, Naucratius changed the whole direction of his life. Nyssen tells us: "By some divine foresight he despised all these things he already had in hand, and, through some great inspiration of thought, went off to a life of solitude and voluntary poverty."[12]

Having reached the very threshold of worldly advancement, Naucratius abandoned these prospects and chose a life of ascetic retreat. Certainly, his choice was informed by the faith and religious commitment that were encouraged and modeled by Macrina. In addition, Naucratius may have faced an especially troubling discord between the career options available to him and the deeply held commitments and values for which his parents and grandparents had become refugees and to which his mother, sister, and big brother dedicated their lives.

Naucratius came of age while Constantinius II ruled the Eastern Empire. As mentioned in chapter 5, this son of Constantine responded to unrest with an aggressive expansion of the Roman imperial administration and army in the region. Bureaucrats, clerks, court advocates, and military officers were urgently needed, and educated Roman citizens from the Mediterranean were not exactly flooding into cold, remote Asia Minor to fill these positions. As a result, many opportunities for potentially prestigious and lucrative careers were available to educated sons of the local aristocracy. A young man like Naucratius would have been recruited

---

12. Gregory of Nyssa, *Life of Macrina* (trans. Silvas), 119.

heavily. He showed great physical ability, quickness in learning, aptitude in application, and the capacity to move and motivate people. Could there be a more desirable candidate to shape as an officer of the imperial army? And, in that time and place, could a young man find a career with more potential for glory, power, and wealth? At the same time, of course, this would mean serving the occupying empire and imposing its will on the people of his own region.

Furthermore, the choice Naucratius faced was not as simple as just deciding to join the army or stay home. If he stayed on the family estate trying to continue the traditional life of his family, he would face imperial taxation officials. With eldest son Basil away in Athens preparing for an illustrious career, second son Naucratius might well find himself saddled with the burden of extracting from his neighbors and his own estates the grain, livestock, textiles, stone, lumber, and slave laborers that the empire demanded. In doing this, he would reduce his family's resources and further impoverish the already poor peasants who worked the land. He would face this scenario not only at their home base of Annisa but on family estates in three different provinces, dealing with three different imperial governors and at least as many tax assessors and collectors.

A bright, educated, devout, and loyal young man in Naucratius's situation might well feel some hesitation. Did he talk it over with Macrina and Emmelia? There is no record of such a conversation, but if he did, his sister and mother, who were immersed in lives of faith and also clear-eyed and savvy business-women, might have advised the course he chose. Whatever his reasoning, his decision was in step with the people who joined the desert ascetic movement around that same time—except that Naucratius did not go to the desert: he set out to become that rare Cappadocian ascetic hermit.

> He took nothing with him but himself, except that one of the house-servants named Chrysaphius followed him, because he was accustomed to attending him and had determined on the same choice of life.[13]

Naucratius and Chrysaphius found a retreat by the Iris River, which winds through Asia Minor, from the mountains of Armenia to the Black Sea. Hidden in the overhanging hollow of a mountain ridge, they chose a spot thickly covered by deep forest and, as Nyssen explains, "there he

---

13. Gregory of Nyssa, *Life of Macrina* (trans. Silvas), 119.

settled, far from the disturbances of the city and the distractions that come from either military service or the rhetoric of the law courts."[14]

Free from "the din that commonly besets human life,"[15] Naucratius ordered his days with moderation, focused on philosophy and wisdom, and took upon himself the labor of looking after a group of elderly and disabled people who lived together in poverty. A skilled hunter and an athletic young man, he went on hunting expeditions to provide food for these people "while taming his own youth at the same time by such exercises." When Emmelia asked anything of him, he spared no effort in meeting her request. Naucratius lived this hard, pure existence for five years, making his mother, and no doubt his sister, very happy, spending all his powers to support and join their dedication to living the gospel.

Then, at age twenty-seven, he was abruptly and shockingly killed in a fishing accident. Nyssen tells us: "Having set out on the hunt by which he provided necessaries for his old people, he was brought back home a corpse."[16] His companion Chrysaphius also died. Nazianzen wrote three epigrams about Naucratius's tragic death:

> Naucratius was once freeing his fishing-net from a sunken rock in the roaring eddies of the river. The net he did not free, but was caught himself. Tell me, O Word, how the net landed the fisherman, Naucratius, an example of pure life, instead of fish. As I conjecture, both grace and death came to him from the water.
>
> Naucratius died in the eddy of the envious river, entangled in the toils of his sunken net, so that, mortal, thou mayst know the tricks of this life, from which this fleet-footed colt was removed.
>
> Naucratius, caught in the fetters of his net, was released from the fetters of this life by fishing.[17]

Emmelia may have been inspecting a distant estate at the time of the accident—she was three day's journey away. When someone told her the terrible news, she fell on the spot, overcome with grief. Beside her, Macrina met the tragedy with a strength born of deep and living faith:

> She both kept herself from collapse and became the stay of her mother's weakness, raising her up again from the abyss of grief . . .

---

14. Gregory of Nyssa, *Life of Macrina* (trans. Silvas), 119.
15. Gregory of Nyssa, *Life of Macrina* (trans. Silvas), 119.
16. Gregory of Nyssa, *Life of Macrina* (trans. Silvas), 120.
17. Henderson, *Greek Anthology*, Books 7–8, Epigrams 156–158, 467–69.

the lofty and noble soul of the virgin was then more manifest than ever . . . for it was not only a brother but her dearest brother who had been snatched away by this manner of death.[18]

Macrina did not express her grief in wailing, tearing her clothes, or ranting her devastation. She did not compose poems of pain or sing laments. Instead, she offered what Nyssen calls "reasonings" to sustain herself and her mother. There was fear that Emmelia might be lost. Her family saw her at the threshold of giving way to irreversible despair and watched anxiously for signs that she might find the thread of faith and hope again. Macrina, also in grief, "raised up her mother together with herself by her reasonings, and placed her [mother] beyond all passion, guiding her by her own example to steadfastness and courage."[19]

What did Macrina say to her mother? A possible rendering of her wisdom follows. (As discussed in the introduction, this is the author's interpretation and paraphrase, drawing mainly from *On the Soul and the Resurrection*, translations by Roth and Silvas.)

Interpretation of Macrina's Wisdom for Her Grieving Mother

Even though we feel nothing but pain right now, God is still here, still holding us in creation with all its wonders. The cosmos is still speaking without words. If we listen with our hearts, the music of the spheres is still around us, still resonating within us, still singing the presence of God.

We need not be afraid of death, or feel grief on behalf of the dead, for we are souls that abide forever, and the Lord has given us the great hope of the resurrection.

Death is not the end of our being—it is only a dividing point between our embodied life and our bodiless life. In death, this bodily covering dissolves, but the spiritual body will be woven again, in the resurrection, of a fiber spun of something more subtle. We will find that everything we love comes back to us in brighter and more beautiful form.

In death we will come back together with our true self—with our original, divinely formed nature. We are created good, and in the fullness of God's love, given the power to choose what we do and how we live. If we have chosen well in life, in death we

---

18. Gregory of Nyssa, *Life of Macrina* (trans. Silvas), 120.
19. Gregory of Nyssa, *Life of Macrina* (trans. Silvas), 120.

flow easily into unity with our true and essential being, and we are free. Then the only thing left is love. The only thing left is to be absorbed in, and filled with, the enjoyment of present and ongoing blessings.

Naucratius prepared well in life, and in death he has entered upon his true life, received into the embrace of the beloved.

Still, do not be discouraged or upset with yourself when you find yourself clinging to the earthly body of your loved one and devastated by the loss of his bodily presence. God is here, completely with us, even while we are overcome with grief at being unyoked from what we have loved in this life. Even when we are flooded with anguish, God is here offering us the basis and the possibility of hope.

Macrina made hope real by applying herself to, and carrying her mother in, full daily practice and vocational work. They were occupied with active forms of devotion, generosity, mercy, justice, and humility so that, from the beauty of this lived experience, Emmelia was lifted out of despondency and could begin to "rejoice instead at the blessings she saw before her."[20]

Meditation

Pause to still and center yourself. Is there a passage from Macrina's wisdom that captured your attention? If so, meditate on that and, for Scripture meditation, consider Jas 4:14, Matt 6:25–34, or Luke 12:22–32. Read your chosen passage three times, as before, first to understand the words, second with attention to your own response, and third to hold the Scripture in prayerful readiness to anything the Spirit may open to you.

---

20. Gregory of Nyssa, *Life of Macrina* (trans. Silvas), 121.

8

Macrina and Basil: Brother and Sister in Faith

"Make my joy complete: be of the same mind, having the same love, being in full accord and of one mind. Do nothing from selfish ambition or conceit, but in humility regard others as better than yourself." (Phil 2:1–3)

SILENCE IN THE HISTORICAL records veils Macrina's relationship with her famous brother St. Basil the Great. Indeed, much has been made of the fact that Basil does not mention Macrina by name in any of his extant writings. Contemporary Western authors tend to see this as a sign that he chose to disregard and ignore his remarkable sister, and some authors have speculated about possible motives such as sibling rivalry, harbored resentments, or prideful inability to give credit due.[1] As discussed in the introduction, these interpretations are questionable at best. Basil's silence honored Macrina's charism, which was a spirituality of inward transcendence made possible through hiddenness. As Nyssen put it, to be unknown was her fame.[2] She chose to be unseen so that she could pray, work, and live with God as her reference-point. Through hiddenness, she sought freedom from worldly vanity, from anxiety for approval, and from the fear of losing the love of others.

---

1. Van Dam, *Families and Friends in Late Roman Cappadocia*, 18–29.
2. Gregory of Nyssa, *Life of Saint Macrina* (trans. Corrigan), 30.

While there are many things we do not know about their relationship, Macrina and Basil were certainly important to each other. In reading of their lives, what emerges, in my view at least, is not siblings estranged or at odds, but a brother and sister deeply dedicated in faith and working in parallel, and sometimes in concert, for the same goals and with the same values.

Although Basil was born less than two years after Macrina, their early experiences differed considerably. Unlike Macrina, infant Basil received the normal form of care for children in aristocratic families—he was assigned to a nurse who was his primary caregiver. A relative within the extended family, she was his wet-nurse in infancy, nanny in early childhood, and an important mother figure while he was growing up. From a modern perspective this may appear as a negative for Basil, as being put aside by his mother.[3] For his family, however, the arrangement was likely seen as giving him the most and the best. Mother Emmelia's choice to breastfeed and care for Macrina herself was a rare departure from the normal child-rearing practices of the day, occasioned by the spiritual bond formed through her childbed vision, and possible because there were not yet other children needing attention. Emmelia went on to birth another baby every twenty-two months (on average) for eighteen years. All these babies needed to be cared for in a world with high infant mortality rates and without time-saving modern conveniences such as, say, running water, washing machines, formula and bottles to fall back on in case of infant feeding problems, and so on. Providing a private nurse for a baby was not an act of neglect or disinterest: it was the way to give the baby his greatest chance of surviving and thriving—the best nutrition and the most attentive and dedicated care. Basil, indeed, later expressed warm appreciation for his nurse and her own son who was like a brother in his early years.

Further separating Basil and Macrina's early experience, boys and girls were raised differently in the gender-stratified culture of the ancient Near East—their daily activities, privileges, and the content of their instruction were largely distinct. As eldest son and heir, Basil was given education and privileges (and a burden of expectations) greater than any of his siblings. There may have been times when he and Macrina were together for prayer or perhaps for instruction from their mother and grandmother, but most of their time was spent apart: as a boy, Basil was not learning to work in wool, and he was not expected to care for younger siblings or help his mother

---

3. Van Dam, *Families and Friends in Late Roman Cappadocia*, 19.

and grandmother with their daily activities. He was not confined to the company of the adult women of his home. When he was not engaged in lessons with Emmelia or Macrina the Elder, he was free to range around the estates, play with other boys, perhaps learn masculine skills from male tutors, or join male relatives in men's activities.

In the writings of his family and friends, the young Basil appears as a fiercely talented boy, although perhaps never an easy personality. He was gifted with uncommon powers of intellect, analysis, and argumentation. In adult life, his commitment to religious discipline was unstinting: he devoted great efforts to helping the poor, and he shrank from *nothing* in defending the faith. At the same time, in interactions with others, he sometimes seemed proud, overbearing, or unsympathetic.

Basil's edgy qualities were no doubt amplified by the health problems with which he contended throughout his life. His chronic bouts of fatigue, fever, and excessive weight loss have led some historians to conjecture that Basil suffered from Crohn's disease.[4] In a letter to fellow bishops, probably written during his early- to mid-forties, Basil said, "you know well how, from my early manhood to my present old age, this ailment has been my constant companion, brought up with me, and chastising me."[5] In another letter, he wrote, "Once more my complaints have come back to me; once more I am confined to my bed, tossing about in my weakness, and every hour all but looking for the end of life . . ."[6] And later, "I have been so wasted by constant and violent attacks of fever that there does seem something thinner even than I was—I am thinner than ever . . . I am in such a feeble state that I am no stronger than a cobweb."[7]

Around the age of a present-day junior high student, Basil attended his father's school for perhaps two or three years. When Basil the Elder died, Macrina seems to have stepped into an almost parental role in his life, applying herself alongside Emmelia to support his education and take care of home responsibilities that might otherwise have distracted and burdened him as eldest son and male head of the family. We saw in the previous chapter that, once settled at Annisa, Basil and the other older boys attended a school in Caesarea. When he was about twenty (349 CE), he went on to Constantinople which, as the new imperial capital, was home

---

4. Van Dam, *Families and Friends in Late Roman Cappadocia*, 37, 198–99.
5. Basil of Caesarea, *Complete Works*, Letter 203, Loc 9375.
6. Basil of Caesarea, *Complete Works*, Letter Thirty, Loc 6051.
7. Basil of Caesarea, *Complete Works*, Letter 193, Loc 9141.

to many distinguished teachers of philosophy and rhetoric. The following year, he continued to Athens where he studied under some of the greatest minds of his time for five or six years. He excelled in this setting and, according to his close friend and companion Nazianzen, became master of "all the learning attainable by the nature of man."[8]

Rather suddenly, in early summer 356, Basil left his studies in Athens and, despite attempts to persuade him to stay on, hurried back to Annisa. This journey may have been prompted by Naucratius's tragic death.[9] After spending some time with the family, Basil went to his former school in Caesarea, where he taught rhetoric for a brief period.

Nyssen, then about twenty-one, was still a student there and studied with Basil during this time. He later commented on the value of the instruction he received: "I enjoyed my brother's society only for a short time, and got only just enough polish from his diviner tongue to be able to discern the ignorance of those who are uninitiated in oratory."[10] At the same time, Basil's difficult qualities were also in evidence back at his own school: "He was at that time excessively puffed up with the thought of his own eloquence and was disdainful of local dignitaries, since in his own inflated opinion he surpassed all the leading luminaries."[11]

Macrina, who was grieving Naucratius and supporting Emmelia in her grief, also acted as a mentor/parental figure in giving the proud young Basil a course correction: "She took him in hand and drew him with such speed toward the goal of philosophy that he withdrew from the worldly show and despised the applause to be gained through eloquence, and went over of his own accord to the life of [poverty and manual labor], thus providing for himself through prefect renunciation a life that would lead without impediment to virtue."[12] What did Macrina say to her brother to bring him around so quickly? There is no direct record of their conversation, but based on Nyssen's retelling of her teachings, I offer a possible interpretation (again, the author's composition drawing from original sources):

---

8. Schaff, *Sketch of the Life and Works of St. Basil*, Loc 217.
9. Silvas, *Macrina the Younger*, 35.
10. Gregory of Nyssa, *Collection, Letter Ten to Libanius*, Loc 10204.
11. Gregory of Nyssa, *Life of Macrina* (trans. Silvas), 117.
12. Gregory of Nyssa, *Life of Macrina* (trans. Silvas), 117.

A PURE MIRROR TURNED TO FACE THE SUN

Interpretation of Macrina's Wisdom
for Brother Basil

My brother, we are souls created to manifest the likeness of God, but we are not the same as God. Just as a mirror holds the image of the person standing before it, our souls are made to hold the image of God. Our greatest possibility, the true purpose of our lives, and the meaning of faith is to hold within ourselves the likeness of God—to mirror our divine prototype—as nearly as we can, in every aspect and every moment of our living and being in this life.

While this is the constant aim of the follower of Christ, even if a human being could really become "a spotless mirror of the working of God and image of his goodness" (Wis 7:26), he would be no more exalted than a fragment of glass that reflects a tiny impression of the sun: the circle of the sun may be captured in this slight fragment, but the sun cannot be held there in the fullness of its real size, heat, brilliance, and power. Likewise, at our best, the ineffable qualities of deity can shine forth in us only slightly, according to the slightness of our nature.

Among the ways we can act as mirrors of the divine, the arts are especially direct expressions of the soul. The wisdom of the soul is the source and substance of all our skills, technical powers, and creative inspirations. My brother, your great art and skill are your soul in action, but how you use these gifts is in your own hands. In God's boundless love for us, he has given us the freedom to choose whether to do what is good or what is worse. When we choose what is good, we faithfully mirror our divine archetype and are at one with our true and essential nature. When we choose what is worse, we divide ourselves from our true nature, turn our glass-fragment selves away from the sun, and no longer see or hold the light.

Where desire and anger govern our actions, we risk losing the light. These emotions are neither good nor bad in themselves. Indeed, emotions are essential to our progress: without desire, what would draw us toward union with the heavenly? If affection were removed from our nature, in what would we be united with God? Without anger, where would we find the courage to stand up for what is right? Without fear, what would give us prudent caution? But we must make humble and diligent efforts to use the energy of our emotions to grow closer to the beautiful, to what is good, and not let them lead us into error. For too easily, anger gives rise to contempt and aggression. Too often, desire joins with these to spawn an ignominious appetite for dominance, vengeance, and conquest.

To choose what is good, each of us must take care in discerning the difference between the bad and the beautiful, between the fulfillment found in true virtue and the illusory pleasures gained through pride and indulgence. Our brother Naucratius chose the good by freeing himself from destructive passions arising from ungoverned anger and desire. In life, he found true freedom and peace in surrender of all else except love of God. When he crossed into disembodied life, I am certain that he was easily reunited with his true, created nature. Like Lazarus (Luke 16:19–31) carried to the bosom of Abraham, he is now in the embrace of the beloved, immersed in the holy good.

My brother, let us also choose the good. Let us join Naucratius in releasing disordered passions. Let us direct our appetites and emotions in the path of wisdom. If we have gifts of skill, intellect, or technical power, let us use them in the image, in imitation, of the Lord.

Basil's preserved writings contain no mention of Macrina's influence on him, but he later wrote, "Much time I had spent in vanity, and had wasted nearly all my youth . . . Then once upon a time, like a man roused from deep sleep, I turned my eyes to the marvelous light of the truth of the Gospel . . . I wept tears over my miserable life and I prayed that guidance might be vouchsafed me . . ."[13]

At this turning point in his life, Basil made up his mind to go to Eustathius of Sebasteia (a leader of early monastic communities who taught a rather extreme form of asceticism), but his journey was delayed by bouts of illness. It was perhaps spring 357 when he was well enough to set out. He traveled around the Near East but kept missing Eustathius, who left each city just before Basil arrived. After missing Eustathius in Alexandria, Basil decided to stay there for a while, talking with religious leaders and observing desert ascetics in Egypt. He also visited desert fathers in Palestine during his travels. After about a year, he went home to Annisa to commit himself to living the gospel through ascetic practice.

Of course, the home to which Basil returned was the already-established ascetic community that Macrina had formed and still led. He lived in a retreat on the estate, leaving the villa to the women's community but

---

13. Basil of Caesarea, *Complete Works*, Letter 223, Loc 10030.

sharing in daily prayer and practice with Macrina, Emmelia, and the women of their household. Later, in Letter 210 he wrote of Annisa:

> I dwelt here for the most part when, fleeing the disturbances of civic life and realizing that this region was a suitable place in which to philosophize because of the tranquility and its solitude, I passed a period of many successive years here, and because of my siblings who even now make this region their home, I found a brief breathing spell from my pressing engagements and have come gladly [back] to this retreat . . .[14]

As Silvas points out, Basil's ideas about women ascetics were certainly formed by his experiences with his mother and sister and their community at Annisa. He became a champion of these women philosophers of faith: "The female too joins the campaign at Christ's side, being enrolled thanks to her virility of soul, rejected in no way for weakness of body. Many women have excelled not one whit less than men. Indeed some have proved themselves even more outstanding."[15]

Intriguing glimpses of Macrina and her community, and of Basil's relationship with her, may also be found in certain material where, without naming names, he wrote about people whose relationships and circumstances exactly corresponded to those of his family. One such example is found in his Letter 46, "To a Fallen Virgin." Possibly, this fallen virgin was a younger sister who had first decided to join the vowed women philosophers of Christ at Annisa, and then changed her mind and eloped with a suitor. The letter is an emphatic—from a modern perspective quite heavy-handed—exhortation to the young woman to return to the ascetic community. Basil urges:

> Recall your grandmother, grown old in Christ but still youthful and vigorous in virtue, and your mother vying with her in the Lord and struggling by strange and unfamiliar labours to break the force of habit, and your sister, who likewise imitates them both, and yet strives even to surpass them for indeed she, by the greater prize of virginity outstrips the achievements of her forebears. Both by her word and by her life, she earnestly summons you . . . Recall these, and the angelic choir around God with them, the spiritual life in the flesh and the heavenly citizenship on earth (cf. Philippians 3.20). Recall the days free of tumult, the illuminated nights,

---

14. Silvas, *Macrina the Younger*, 75.
15. Silvas, *Macrina the Younger*, 61.

the spiritual songs, the resounding psalmody, the holy prayers, the undefiled bed, the frugal table, and the procession of virgins.[16]

Showing perhaps even more clearly his esteem of his sister, Basil established, with little brother Peter, a men's house of ascetic seekers parallel to Macrina and Emmelia's house of women. In Letter 207, which is discussed in more detail below, Basil gives another peek into life in the community at Annisa:

> . . . the people rise early in the night to go to the house of prayer, and in labor and affliction and in continual tears confessing to God, they at length rise from their prayers and commence the psalmody. And at one time indeed they divide into two groups and sing the psalms, alternating between the one and the other, both thereby strengthening their meditation of the scriptural phrases and securing from themselves both their close attention and the means of keeping their hearts from distraction. And then again, after entrusting one to lead the chant, the rest sing in response. And so they pass the night in a variety of psalmody, praying in the intervals. Then as day begins to dawn, all of them in common raise with one voice and one heart the psalm of confession to the Lord [Psalm 51], each of them making his own the words of repentance.[17]

While at Annisa, Basil applied his analytic brilliance to studying the workings of the community of faith, and he began to write out rules to guide such life. He developed these into the Rule of Saint Basil, from which, in Sixth Century Italy, St. Benedict of Nursia would draw heavily in writing the Holy Rule of St. Benedict, which was, in turn, adapted or adopted to guide the organization, practice, and daily life of almost every Western monastic order through the centuries.

After about two years of full-time residence at Annisa, Basil left that sanctuary to step into an active role in the fervent disputes over faith and power that were ablaze in the church and the empire. For years to come he spoke and wrote tirelessly, defining, articulating, and defending the foundations of Christian faith as it is still known and practiced today. Among the controversies into which Basil entered were major disputes about the nature of Christ and of the Trinity.

---

16. Silvas, *Macrina the Younger*, 67–68.
17. Silvas, *Macrina the Younger*, 76–77.

The Trinity, of course, consists of God, the Son, and the Holy Spirit. While this is easy enough to say, further definition of the Trinity baffles logic and deductive reason: there are three and they are all one, each of the three is itself, they are not one another, they are each God, and there is one God. These seemingly contradictory, impossible statements are often approached as an intellectual puzzle to be solved, and both ancient and contemporary thinkers have tried to find solutions. One such thinker was Arius, a Christian who lived in Alexandria (the home city of Origen and Athanasius, near the desert hermitage of St. Anthony) from 256–336 CE. He resolved the logical conundrum of the Trinity by redefining its members: he said there is one transcendent God and, thus, the Son could not also be God but had to be a creature that did not exist until he was created out of nothing by God: "we say that the Son has a beginning, but that God is without beginning."[18] By this argument, Arius redefined Christ as something less that divine—a creature, albeit a perfect and sinless one with unique powers. His solution to the logical puzzle of the Trinity was not welcomed by fellow bishops. Indeed, around 318 a council of one hundred bishops came together to condemn him as a heretic and throw him out of the church. Although banished, Arius did not give up—he continued to make his argument and won the support of an influential bishop, Eusebius of Nicomedia, who took him in and promoted his views. The Council of Nicaea was, as we have seen, called together in 325 (four or five years before Basil was born) by Emperor Constantine. It produced the Nicene Creed, the distilled and unified statement of faith still recited by Christians today, which identifies Jesus Christ as: "the only Son of God, eternally begotten of the Father, God from God, Light from Light, true God form true God, begotten, not made, of one Being with the Father." Despite the work of the Council of Nicaea, however, controversies about the nature and the members of the Trinity, and about wording of the creed, continued for many years.

Although many great minds have tangled with the Trinity as a challenge of reason, it did not originate as an intellectual construct. The idea of the Trinity could not have been derived from any logical analysis of doctrines; rather, the Trinity reflects the remarkable and compelling lived-experience of the earliest Christians. The first Christians, the apostles, knew God (YHWH) throughout their lives, within and through their Jewish communities. They experienced Jesus as God completely, imminently,

---

18. Meister and Stump, *Christian Thought*, 139.

and undeniably (John 20:28). They were transformed by the Holy Spirit, which came to them as the immediate and real presence of God on Pentecost (Acts 2:17). The Trinity reflects "the profound experience Christians attributed to the work of the three members of the Trinity in their lives and among their religious communities."[19] The Trinity, then, carries and holds within it the transcendent experience from which Christianity was born, and it was this that Basil rose to champion.

In a letter to his brother Nyssen, Basil wrote: ". . . it is in nowise possible to entertain the idea of severance or division, in such a way as that the Son should be thought of apart from the Father, or the Spirit be disjoined from the Son. But the communion and the distinction apprehended in [the members of the Trinity] are, in a certain sense, ineffable and inconceivable . . ."[20] In this letter he goes on to draw a beautiful analogy, likening the members of the Trinity to the colors in a rainbow, which appear distinct and yet share the same nature, "the essence emitting the many-coloured radiance, and refracted by the sunbeam, [is] one essence; it is the colour of the phenomenon which is multiform."[21] At the same time, Basil cautions Nyssen regarding the inevitable imperfection of using analogies to capture divine truth: "receive what I say as at best a token and reflection of the truth; not as the actual truth itself. For it is not possible that there should be complete correspondence between what is seen in the tokens and the objects in reference to which the use of tokens is adopted."[22]

Basil's arguments on the nature of Trinity and the divinity of God, Christ, and the Holy Spirit were not made within a rarified and peaceable ivory tower setting—this controversy excited society broadly, and the powerful especially. Basil contended against fellow bishops, clergy, imperial officials, and in some instances, against reigning emperors. An especially dramatic confrontation took place between Basil and Emperor Valens and his recently-converted and newly-appointed prefect of the East, Modestus. Nyssen and Nazianzen both tell the story. In setting the stage, Nyssen explains that Valens was won over to doctrinal positions opposing the Nicene faith held by Basil and his family and friends. Some people shared Valens's point of view,

---

19. Meister and Stump, *Christian Thought*, 164.
20. Basil of Caesarea, *Complete Works, Letter Thirty-eight*, Loc 6209.
21. Basil of Caesarea, *Complete Works, Letter Thirty-eight*, Loc 6235.
22. Basil of Caesarea, *Complete Works, Letter Thirty-eight*, Loc 6215.

A PURE MIRROR TURNED TO FACE THE SUN

... while others, and they were the majority, were ready from fear to indulge the imperial pleasure, and seeing the severity employed against those who held the Faith were ostentatious in their zeal for [Valens]. It was a time of exile, confiscation, banishment, threats of fines, danger of life, arrests, imprisonment, scourging; nothing was too dreadful to put in force against those who would not yield to this sudden caprice of the Emperor.[23]

Nazianzen tells of Valens and Modestus using "open and secret plots, persuasion, where time allowed, violence, where persuasion was impossible"[24] to bring the churches of the empire into submission under their doctrine. Those who held to the orthodox faith were thrown out of their churches and replaced with clergy who followed the emperor. There were rumors that Modestus put eighty opposing clerics on a ship and burned it at sea. Blood was shed in churches. In early 370, Valens sent Modestus to confront Basil with a demand that he disavow the Nicene Creed. According to Nazianzen, Cappadocia was at that point the only quarter in which church leaders had not capitulated to the imperial revision of doctrine.

Modestus approached Basil with "mingled threats and promises, royal favors and ecclesiastical power to obedience." Basil responded by explaining that these tactics "could not succeed with men who cared only for the empire of Christ, and the Powers that never die . . ."[25] When Modestus threatened him, Basil told him that "[even] the endurance of blows, or tortures, or death if it might be for the Truth, was an object not of fear, not even to women, but to every Christian it was the supremest bliss to suffer the worst for this was their hope, and they were only grieved that nature allowed them but one death, and that they could devise no means of dying many times in this battle for the Truth."[26]

Nyssen describes Modestus then shifting tactics "like those rapid changes on the stage when one mask after another is put on"[27] and turning instead to flattering Basil and trying to persuade him gently—he did not even need to abandon the Nicene Creed—Modestus and the Emperor would be satisfied if he would just agree to smallest revision: removal of a single word.

---

23. Gregory of Nyssa, *Collection, Against Eunomius*, Loc 3108.
24. Gregory of Nazianzus, *Collection, Select Orations*, Loc 8349.
25. Gregory of Nyssa, *Collection, Against Eunomius*, Loc 3137–144.
26. Gregory of Nyssa, *Collection, Against Eunomius*, Loc 3137–144.
27. Gregory of Nyssa, *Collection, Against Eunomius*, Loc 3144.

The word they had in mind, homoousias, is translated in English as "of one being with." As in, "begotten, not made, of one being with the Father." This word was, of course, at the very heart of the question in the Trinitarian controversies—was the Son of the same being with the Father or was he a creature created by the Father? Was Christ, the Son, of the divine being, or was he something else, perhaps a sort of demi-god? Basil responded, saying that he would never consider changes, even in the order of the written words of the creed, let alone additions to or subtractions from the Faith.

Modestus's next tactic was to bring Basil to court for a sort of trial. Now this would have been a very public confrontation between powerful men—the emperor's prefect and a metropolitan Bishop. Modestus and his court were likely arrayed with all the accoutrements of power and prestige—fine attire, insignia of rank, braces of soldiers at hand. Basil, on the other hand, followed ascetic principles which prescribed, essentially, a monk's attire. He taught that the Christian should keep only the minimum clothing necessary to protect the body against "mischief from the air"[28] and provide decency, and should not violate the principle of poverty by any luxury such as keeping "some garments to wear in public and others for use at home, nor, again some to be worn in the day time, others at night, but we should contrive to have only one garment which can serve all occasions."[29] When summoned to this public showdown with Modestus, Basil was likely dressed in worn and simple garb and, while only in his forties, he was prematurely gaunt and frail-looking because of his chronic illness. Nazianzen describes the events of that day:

> Our noble prelate [Basil] was brought into or rather entered his court, as if bidden to a feast instead of a trial. How can I fully describe, either the arrogance of the prefect or the prudence with which it was met?
>
> "What is the meaning, Sir Basil," he said, addressing him by name and not as yet deigning to term him Bishop, "of your daring, as no other dares, to resist and oppose so great a potentate?"
>
> "In what respect?" said our noble champion, "and in what does my rashness consist? For this I have yet to learn."
>
> "In refusing to respect the religion of your Sovereign, when all others have yielded and submitted themselves."

---

28. Basil of Caesarea, *Complete Works, Long Rules 22*, Loc 15232.
29. Basil of Caesarea, *Complete Works, Long Rules 22*, Loc 15233.

"Because," said he, "this is not the will of my real Sovereign; nor can I, who am the creature of God, and bidden myself to be God, submit to worship any creature."

"And what do we," said the prefect, "seem to you to be? Are we who give this injunction, nothing at all, what do you say to this? Is it not a great thing to be ranged with us as your associates?"

"You are, I will not deny it," said he, "a prefect, and an illustrious one, yet not of more honor than God. And to be associated with you is a great thing, certainly; for you are yourself the creature of God; but so it is to be associated with any other of my subjects. For faith, and not personal importance, is the distinctive mark of Christianity."

Then indeed the prefect became excited, and rose from his seat, boiling with rage, and making use of harsher language. "What?" said he, "have you no fear of my authority?"

"Fear of what?" said Basil, "How could it affect me?"

"Of what? Of any one of the resources of my power."

"What are these?" said Basil, "Pray inform me."

"Confiscation, banishment, torture, death."

"Have you no other threat?" said he, "for none of these can reach me . . . a man who has nothing is beyond the reach of confiscation; unless you demand my tattered rags, and the few books, which are my only possessions. Banishment is impossible for me, who am confined by no limit of place, counting my own neither the land where I now dwell, nor all of that into which I may be hurled; or rather, counting it all God's, whose guest and dependent I am. As for tortures, what hold can they have upon one whose body has ceased to be? Unless you mean the first stroke, for this alone is in your power. Death is my benefactor, for it will send me the sooner to God, for Whom I live, and exist, and have all but died, and to Whom I have long been hastening."[30]

Modestus's belligerent manner was replaced with a degree of respect and deference and he dismissed Basil from his court and went to the emperor where, according to Nazianzen, he explained, "We have been worsted, Sire . . . we must make trial of some more feeble character; and in [Basil's] case resort to open violence, or submit to the disregard of our threats."[31] Emperor Valens heard high praises of Basil and decided against open

---

30. Gregory of Nazianzus, *Collection, Oration XLIII Funeral of Great St. Basil*, Loc 8369-389.

31. Gregory of Nazianzus, *Collection, Oration XLIII Funeral of Great St. Basil*, Loc 8392.

violence against him. Instead, he went with his whole train to Basil's church to take his place among the people and make a showing of unity.

> Upon his entrance he was struck by the thundering roll of the Psalms, by the sea of the heads of the congregation, and by the angelic rather than human order which pervaded the sanctuary and its precincts; while Basil presided over his people, standing erect, as the Scripture says of Samuel, with body and eyes and mind undisturbed, as if nothing new had happened, but fixed upon God and the sanctuary, as if, so to say, he had been a statue, while his ministers stood around him in fear and reverence.[32]

The emperor was overwhelmed and shaken by "human weakness, his eyes were affected with dimness and giddiness, his mind with dread."[33] When he went to altar to present the gifts to the Table of God, as required in the liturgy, he staggered, and would have fallen except that someone in the sanctuary reached out to steady him. After this, the emperor relented, at least in large degree, in his persecution of the Cappadocian Christians. Basil, however, knew little rest—challenges and controversies continued, and he battled on:

> After a period of such recollection as was possible, and private spiritual conference, in which, after considering all human arguments, and penetrating into all the deep things of the Scriptures, he drew up a sketch of the pious doctrine, and by wrestling with and attacking their opposition he beat off the daring assaults of the heretics: overthrowing in hand to hand struggles by word of mouth those who came to close quarters, and striking those at distance by arrows winged with ink . . .[34]

While Basil faced down emperors and fought off heretics, he also watched over his family at Annisa, where Macrina, Peter, and Emmelia carried on, living in and leading their faith communities. In Letter 207, written from Annisa, Basil is addressing the Clergy of Neocaesaria concerning accusations and derogatory claims that were being made against the community at Annisa and against himself. He begins with these words:

> The unanimity of your hatred against us and the fact that to a man you all follow him who heads the war against us, induced me to keep silent with all alike, and neither to begin a friendly

32. Gregory of Nazianzus, *Collection, Oration XLIII Funeral of Great St. Basil*, Loc 8399.
33. Gregory of Nazianzus, *Collection, Oration XLIII Funeral of Great St. Basil*, Loc 8402.
34. Gregory of Nazianzus, *Collection, Oration XLIII Funeral of Great St. Basil*, Loc 8323.

correspondence nor any communication, but calmly to nurse my grief. Yet since I ought not to be silent before slanders—not that we may avenge ourselves by contradicting them but that we may not suffer the lie to prosper and may avoid involving in the injury those who have been deceived—it has seemed necessary for me to set this matter before all, and to write to your Intelligence . . .[35]

After some discussion about the motives, tactics, and theological errors of the parties involved in the dispute, Basil goes on to defend the community at Anissa:

> If they are asked the reason for their unproclaimed and truceless war, they mention psalms and a manner of singing which differs from the custom in use among you, and things of this sort for which they ought to feel ashamed. But we are being accused because we have men practiced in piety, who have withdrawn from the world and all earthly cares, which the Lord likens to thorns since they do not permit the word to come to fruitfulness. Such men carry about their bodies the mortification of Jesus, and having taken up their cross are following God. I would count it worth my whole life to have these as my faults, and to have people with me and under me as [their] teacher who have chosen this life of asceticism . . . And if women also choose to live according to the Gospel, and prefer virginity to marriage, by enslaving the arrogance of the flesh, and living in a sorrow which is deemed blessed, they are blessed in their choice wherever they are in the world . . . And if they charge any disorderliness in the life of our women, I do not undertake to apologize for them: but this testimony I do make to you, that what Satan, the father of lies, has not undertaken to say up to this time, these audacious hearts and unbridled mouths are ever voicing unscrupulously. But I desire you to know that we boast of having a body of men and women whose conversation is in heaven, who have crucified their flesh with its affections and desires, who do not concern themselves with food and clothing, but, being undistracted and in constant attendance upon the Lord, remain night and day in prayer. Their mouths do not proclaim the works of men, but they sing hymns to our God unceasingly, while they work with their own hands that they may have something to share with those who have need.[36]

---

35. Basil of Caesarea, *Collection, Letter CCVII*, 578.
36. Basil of Caesarea, *Collection, Letter CCVII*, 579.

Basil's words convey his ongoing commitment to and identity with the community at Annisa. In his early life, Macrina functioned in the roles of parent and mentor, helping him to develop his talent and giving him an effective course-correction when he showed signs of youthful arrogance. Early in his career, he lived beside her established ascetic community and worked alongside her in developing the foundations of Christian monasticism. When he stepped into church leadership, Basil watched over the community at Annisa and, when needed, came to its defense while Macrina carried on the groundwork of building and sustaining a new way of life in a harsh and uncertain world. Macrina dedicated herself to taking "the family's already deeply Christian impulses to a new level with her commitment to virginity and asceticism."[37] At the same time, as Silvas puts it, "Basil's part, through the opportunities of his superb education, his aristocratic social standing, and his commitment to participation in the Church at large, to say nothing of his own extraordinary qualities, was to articulate the spirit of Christian virginity."[38] Through her lived philosophy, Macrina led her people into ascetic lives within the hiddenness of her home-turned-monastery. Basil took upon himself the public and outward work—and danger—of contending with imperial authorities and hostile churchmen. The two were united in their faith, their dedication to living and teaching the gospel, and their ministry to the greater community.

Meditation:

Consider Macrina's wisdom:

> We are souls created to manifest the likeness of God. Just as a mirror holds the image of the person standing before it, our souls are made to hold the image of God. Our greatest possibility, the true purpose of our lives, and the meaning of faith is to hold within ourselves the likeness of God—to mirror our divine prototype—as nearly as we can, in every aspect and every moment of our living and being in this life.

For Scripture meditation, look at Phil 2:5–8; Rom 12:3–18; Matt 5:3–12. Read one or more passage three times, first to understand the words, second with attention to your own response, and third to hold the Scripture in prayerful readiness to anything the Spirit may open to you.

---

37. Silvas, *Macrina the Younger*, 56.
38. Silvas, *Macrina the Younger*, 57.

9

Breast Cancer, Suffering, and Healing

"[Jesus] said to her, 'Daughter, your faith has made you well; go in peace and be healed of your disease.'" (Mark 5:34)

WE DO NOT KNOW when or how Macrina first noticed the lump in her breast. Perhaps tightness or pain drew her hand to the hardness under her skin. Possibly, like many women, she felt nothing at all until a change in the contour of her body caught her eye, or in bathing her hand brushed over a swelling where none had been. Her close friend Vetiana later told Nyssen that "a frightful disease" grew in Macrina's breast, a disease that was "perilous whether the tumor were cut out, or the affliction progressed to a completely incurable state by spreading to the region of the heart."[1]

Physicians in that time knew about breast cancer and even called it by its modern name. The Greek physician Hippocrates had described several types of cancer around 400 BCE (about the time of Plato). Because malignant tumors are firmly attached to surrounding tissues, as if by the arms and claws of a crab, Hippocrates named this disease "the crab," in Greek "cancer." He advised poultices and herbs for treatment of breast cancer. If this did not work, he recommended surgery, and if surgery was unsuccessful, he recommended cautery, or burning the tissue with hot irons to kill the disease. Of course, these things had to be done without modern

---

1. Gregory of Nyssa, *Life of Macrina* (trans. Silvas), 141.

anesthesia, antiseptics, or surgical techniques which, for example, prevent hemorrhage and minimize scarring.

Another ancient Greek physician, Aulus Celsus, who lived around the same time as Jesus, also wrote about breast cancer. He recommended aggressive surgery, but only if the tumors were identified in an early stage. He cautioned that even after removal and healing, breast cancer could return with swelling in the armpit, and cause death.

In the first and second centuries, topical remedies for breast cancer were used by many physicians—poultices of cucumber, figs, milkweed, pennyroyal, mallows, honey, lentils, milk, sesame, plantain, and various other ingredients. Oral preparations such as hot goose blood or asses' blood in water were prescribed. Around this time, use of cautery as way to control bleeding during surgery was described. The surgeon was to cut, apply hot irons until the bleeding stopped, then cut, then burn again—all still without modern anesthesia or sterile equipment, of course. Despite these developments in treatment, physicians such as Cassius Felix and Rufus of Ephesus recorded their opinions that breast cancer could not be cured.

About a hundred and fifty years before Macrina's lifetime, Claudius Galen wrote that breast cancer was the most common form of cancer. He taught that blood-letting could treat breast cancer by ridding the body of excess "black bile." He also advised various topical remedies, and like Hippocrates he recommended surgery and cautery to treat breast cancer in those patients who were not cured by these methods—and were strong enough to endure the procedures.

When Macrina's tumor was discovered, Emmelia very much wanted her to receive medical care. Of course, mother Emmelia's feelings are easy to understand—true, the available cancer treatment was hard and painful, and the outcome was quite uncertain, but letting the cancer take its course would also involve suffering, and the outcome was fairly certain: imminent death. Reasoning that it was surely better to do what could be done, Emmelia tried to persuade her daughter: "Many times her mother begged her and implored her to accept treatment from a physician."[2]

Macrina, however, made the decision to refuse the physician and turn to prayer alone. She directly refused her mother's wish, possibly for the only time, or at least as one of a very few instances, and she turned away from treatment that held at least slight hope of removing the disease. If Macrina's choice was, like her other choices throughout her life, a response to her

2. Gregory of Nyssa, *Life of Macrina* (trans. Silvas), 141.

calling, an expression of her commitment to live wisdom, how did her discernment of calling and wisdom lead to this startling decision? What can we learn about her philosophy from her choice?

In Macrina's society there was active debate about whether Christians should resort to physicians or whether they should seek healing through faith alone. This is a question that is woven all through Christian history and debated in some circles even today. The content of the ancient debate was different from contemporary discussions, however, in that the modern science-versus-religion dichotomy did not yet exist. Disease and healing were generally understood as spiritual processes with physical manifestations. That is, just as most Westerners today understand disease to be caused by physical factors such as germs, genes, and harmful biochemical changes, ancient people understood disease to arise from spiritual dynamics, such as influence by outside harmful spirits (e.g., demons), corruption of the spiritual being by harmful or unhealthy impulses and attachments, or spiritual imbalances or deficiencies of needed qualities such as courage, humility, compassion, self-control, and patience. Healing involved correcting these spiritual pathologies—exorcising demons, purification, and building strengths of the spirit through practices such as fasting and prayer. Taking this understanding of disease another step, some ancient Christians reasoned that seeking treatment from a physician amounted to a failure of faith or a self-indulgent attempt to bypass the hard work of purification and spiritual growth.

Following such reasoning, did Macrina believe that her vocation required that she rely on faith-based healing alone? Nyssen seems to anticipate this question, and he is careful to show that her choice was not based on concerns about the piety of medicine. He tells us that Emmelia reasoned with Macrina, saying that medicine, like other human technologies, "was sent from God for the saving of human beings."[3] This statement also reflects the views of Macrina's family and friends, articulated by Basil in his Long Rules (LR 55). Basil taught that the medical arts are gifts provided by God to remedy our susceptibility to illness and affliction. God gave people the agricultural arts to produce food, he said, and so people do not simply stand in the field praying but rather pray and also farm. Likewise, people use the arts of spinning and weaving to produce fabric rather than limiting themselves to praying for clothing. In the same way, he said, Christians may use the art of medicine along with prayer and

---

3. Gregory of Nyssa, *Life of Macrina* (trans. Silvas), 141.

spiritual practices to remedy illness and injury: "As we entrust the helm to the pilot in the art of navigation, but implore God that we may end our voyage unharmed by the perils of sea, so also, when reason allows, we call in the doctor, but we do not leave off hoping in God."[4]

Basil, who himself struggled with chronic and debilitating illness, taught that decisions about when to call the doctor should, like everything else, be guided by the one great goal of life: living the gospel, mirroring the divine, theosis. As he put it, "whether we follow the precepts of the medical art or decline to have recourse to them . . . we should hold to our objective of pleasing God and see to it that the soul's benefit is assured."[5] Obtaining medical care should be considered in the same way as other choices:

> Whatever requires an undue amount of thought or trouble or involves large expenditures of effort and causes our whole life to revolve, as it were, around the solicitude for the flesh must be avoided by Christians. Consequently, we must take care to employ this medical art, if it should be necessary, not as making it wholly accountable for our state of health or illness, but as redounding to the glory of God and as a parallel to the care given the soul.[6]

Basil argued that physical medicine could be complimentary to spiritual healing and could even serve "as a model for the cure of the soul, to guide us in the removal of what is superfluous and in the addition of what is lacking."[7] For example, ancient medicine taught that bad physical habits, such as eating and drinking too much and too luxuriously, could make the body sick. Then as now, physicians advised people to avoid what is harmful, to limit indulgence, and to partake of the beneficial in activities and in diet. In the same way, Basil explained, spiritual healing involves avoiding harmful, self-serving indulgences and practicing disciplined prayer and spiritual exercise. The transformation of the body from sickness to health through physical intervention is, according to Basil, analogous to the soul's "power to be restored again through penance from its sinful state to its proper integrity."[8] In a comment so closely relevant to Macrina's decision that it might have arisen from conversation with her, he said:

---

4. Basil of Caesarea, *Complete Works*, Long Rules 55, Loc 15926.
5. Basil of Caesarea, *Complete Works*, Long Rules 55, Loc 15934.
6. Basil of Caesarea, *Complete Works*, Long Rules 55, Loc 15872
7. Basil of Caesarea, *Complete Works*, Long Rules 55, Loc 15859.
8. Basil of Caesarea, *Complete Works*, Long Rules 55, Loc 15926.

> Right reason dictates ... that we demur neither at cutting nor at burning, nor at the pains caused by bitter and disagreeable medicines, nor at abstinence from food, nor at a strict regimen, nor at being forced to refrain from that which is hurtful. Nevertheless, we should keep as our objective (again I say it), our spiritual benefit.[9]

Especially pertinent to Macrina's choice is Basil's discussion of certain situations in which application of physical medicine might not benefit the spirit. Perhaps obviously, where physical cures had already been tried and failed and the illness was found to be incurable, he advised that patients focus on growth in faith rather than expending their energies on seeking more doctors and treatments. There are also cases in which acceptance of illness can provide the setting for great growth in spiritual strength, patience, compassion, gratitude, and even discovery of a deep peace. Sometimes patients face and accept incurable illness only to be surprised by a cure that takes place spontaneously, "secretly and without visible means."[10] Either acceptance of illness or unlooked-for cure can turn a patient's attention toward God because they are powerful reminders that, for all our human intelligence and dominance, there are still things beyond our understanding and control.

Two other situations in which medicine was not likely to benefit the spirit were related to demons and sin. If a patient believed that his illness was caused by God as a punishment for sin, Basil advised that health would be restored only through bearing the misery in silence, seeking no relief from medicines, and focusing on penance and atonement. If the affliction came about because of a contest of wills between God and an evil spirit (as is described in the book of Job), the patient's best hope was in confounding the adversary through heroic patience.

There could also be good reasons not to seek medical care in the case that a saint became ill, according to Basil. In the common belief system of that time, only a genuine human being could be afflicted with disease—a spirit or divine being could not. A saint might choose to bear illness without medical care because their affliction proved that they were human and, thus, that their remarkable deeds and special abilities came from faith in Christ rather than some supernatural power of their own. In this way, saints could use their own suffering in sickness to aid in teaching the gospel.

---

9. Basil of Caesarea, *Complete Works*, Long Rules 55, Loc 15902.
10. Basil of Caesarea, *Complete Works*, Long Rules 55, Loc 15874.

In another passage, Basil unfolded an instance in which medical care was not aligned with the work of the spirit through an interpretation of the parable of Lazarus and the rich man. It is interesting that this is the parable Macrina focused on in some of her teachings, which we will explore further in the next chapter. Before delving into Basil's comments on the parable, it perhaps bears saying that this passage of Scripture is a bit difficult—it presents painful and shocking images of human suffering and callous indifference, its lessons are not the easiest to understand, and Basil's interpretation may challenge us as well. The parable is a teaching story, told by Jesus, that begins:

> There was a rich man who was dressed in purple and fine linen who feasted sumptuously every day. And at his gate lay a poor man named Lazarus, covered with sores, who longed to satisfy his hunger with what fell from the rich man's table; even the dogs would come and lick his sores. The poor man died and was carried away by the angels to the bosom of Abraham. The rich man also died and was buried. In Hades, where he was being tormented, he looked up and saw Abraham far away with Lazarus in his bosom. He called out, "Father Abraham, have mercy on me, and send Lazarus to dip the tip of his finger in water and cool my tongue; for I am in agony in these flames." (Luke 16:19–24)

Abraham tells the rich man that this is not possible because a great gulf separates him from Lazarus, preventing either from reaching the other. Besides, Lazarus has already suffered miseries in life while the rich man enjoyed all the good things. The rich man is devastated. As the terrible reality of his life and death come home to him, he pleads: "I beg you to send [Lazarus] to my father's house—for I have five brothers—that he may warn them so that they will not also come into this place of torment." (Luke 16:27). Abraham says that the rich man's brothers already have Moses and the prophets to guide them. The rich man argues that his brothers would pay attention if Lazarus rose from the dead with a personal message for them, but Abraham says that if they won't listen to Moses and prophets, they are not going to listen to Lazarus either, even if he is resurrected.

Basil's interpretation in LR55 frames Lazarus as a special case of the afflicted saint who endures anguish to teach the gospel:

> Then, too, God places those who are able to endure tribulation even unto death before the weak as their model. Lazarus, for example, although afflicted with such painful wounds, never

brought a charge against the rich man, nor made any request of him, nor became peevish at the condition of things; consequently, he came to rest in Abraham's bosom as one who had accepted misfortunes in his lifetime.[11]

Is Basil saying that suffering itself was Lazarus's virtue? Is he telling us that we should emulate this by passively enduring agony and injustice? If his thinking was aligned with Macrina's, this was not quite his point. Macrina said that by this parable, "the Lord seems to be teaching that we who are living in the flesh ought as much as possible to separate and release ourselves from its hold by the life of virtue . . ."[12] This lesson turns on the contrast between the spiritual states of the rich man and Lazarus. As Macrina put it, the rich man is an example of one who has become "wholly and completely fleshly in mind, devoting all movement and energy of the soul to the will of the flesh."[13] Lazarus is an example of those who are free from fleshly attachments and so able to "order their own life here with discerning and sober reasoning, enduring in this brief life things painful to the senses"[14] in order to live a life of virtue and pass into a better eternal life. Basil and Macrina's reading of the parable would have been informed by their parents' experience as refugees. As we saw in chapter 1, Emmelia and Elder Basil began their lives among fugitives of faith who were stripped of every kind of belonging and banished from their homes. They witnessed brutalities, endured great hardship and loss, and lived in danger. Like Lazarus, they knew situations of extremity, yet they did not give way to despair or turn vengeful and violent. Instead, they learned to surrender attachment to everything else except the love and the faith that remained real, sustained them, and could not be taken or destroyed.

In the story, Lazarus is hungry and covered with open sores. He longs to satisfy his hunger, he wants relief, he does not pretend otherwise. Indeed, he sits at the gate, extending to the rich man an open invitation to choose the good, to love his neighbor, to be generous and kind. Instead, the rich man keeps more food than he needs and lets the extra go to waste on the floor. He does nothing to help the poor man even when dogs lick his wounds (in the context of the story, this signaled shocking degradation and humiliation, a man treated as garbage). Through all of this, Lazarus

---

11. Basil of Caesarea, *Complete Works, Long Rules 55*, Loc 15918.
12. Gregory of Nyssa, *On the Soul and the Resurrection* (trans. Roth), 76.
13. Gregory of Nyssa, *On the Soul and the Resurrection* (trans. Silvas), 207.
14. Gregory of Nyssa, *On the Soul and the Resurrection* (trans. Silvas), 205.

shows only acceptance. He does not reject hope by going away to hide. He does not seek confrontation or revenge. He does not undertake to judge or punish or shame the rich man. He simply remains at the gate, present and open to whatever takes place.

Macrina understands Lazarus's response not as pathetic passivity but as an example of gospel life. That is, she treats the parable of Lazarus and rich man as a story through which Jesus offers the same message he taught through his life, death, resurrection: Lazarus knew and accepted suffering at the gate; Jesus knew the trials before him when he prayed at Gethsemane, and he spoke to the Father of both his wish to be spared and his willingness to transcend all his hopes and wishes, saying, "not my will but yours be done" (Luke 22:42). Lazarus was "placed" (as Basil put it) by God at the mercy of other human beings who responded to him with cruel indifference and lethal injustice; Jesus allowed other human beings to take him, place him on trial, and inflict injustice and brutality upon him. Accepting all, even death, Lazarus showed complete surrender, remaining attached only to God; without resistance, Jesus accepted false judgment, torture, humiliation, and "became obedient to the point of death—even death on a cross" (Phil 2:8). Passing into what Macrina spoke of as an "invisible and bodiless state of life,"[15] Lazarus rested in the bosom of Abraham, or "that immeasurable good above."[16] Jesus passed from death to the immeasurable good described as the right hand of the Father, unity in Trinity. The rich man asked Abraham to resurrect Lazarus and send him to tell the living why they should place love and virtue before greed and self-interest, but Abraham said that the living had already been told; if they weren't listening yet, they were not going to listen even if the message was brought by Lazarus risen from the dead. Having prepared his followers with this story and many others, Jesus rose from the dead and remains with us in spirit, and in the teachings of faith and the substance of communion.

Macrina treats Lazarus as one who lived in state of self-transcendent surrender which, within the limitations of his circumstances, freed his soul from distracting impulses and desires so that God was his all in all (1 Cor 15:28). This state is the great aim of all the ascetic traditions. The "immobility" practitioners among the early Jains (chapter 2) set out to surmount karma by sitting still in meditation and absolute surrender through hunger, thirst, pain, physical collapse, and death. Macrina and Basil's parents and their

15. Gregory of Nyssa, *On the Soul and the Resurrection* (trans. Silvas), 206.
16. Gregory of Nyssa, *On the Soul and the Resurrection* (trans. Silvas), 205.

whole generation were forced into conditions of bare survival and grew in faith through loss, danger, and need. The desert fathers and mothers sought surrender by going to the wilderness and creating hardships for themselves so that they could learn freedom from the needs and drives of the body and personality, transcend self, and live for the spirit alone. Macrina practiced radical simplicity, humility, generosity, and hiddenness.

For a person who has attained the self-transcendent state, all of the conditions of life are still experienced fully, and yet they do not direct or determine the state of the soul. There is freedom to choose, based entirely on one's highest beliefs or core values (Macrina used the word virtue); how one will respond to pain and pleasure, hunger and satiety, poverty and wealth, social scorn and esteem, sickness and health; and even prolonged life or imminent death. There is no compulsion to react, no blinding fear, no overwhelming personal need or greed.

In Basil's discussion, saints and exceptional souls are interested in personal happiness and bodily health and comfort only in so far as they aid or hinder life in God. Macrina, in her teachings given to us by Nyssen, embraced both suffering and death as inevitable and essential parts of the soul's journey. At the same time, she expressed no interest in seeking out suffering. She did not see suffering as virtuous in itself, nor as an act of punishment or vengeance by God: "For it is not in hatred, not in retaliation for a life of vice, in my opinion, that God brings upon sinners those painful affects. He is only claiming and drawing to himself whatever by his gift has come into generation."[17] Macrina teaches that our suffering arises "only to separate the good from the bad and to draw [us] into that communion of blessedness."[18] She speaks of suffering as a "purifying fire" that burns away extraneous matter to distill the gold of the soul's true nature. She also uses a grisly analogy that would have been relevant and familiar to people living in ancient Cappadocia:

> [If] the soul is fastened with the nails of passionate attachment to the material state, its case will be something like those of bodies buried beneath the rubble of buildings which have collapsed in earthquakes. Let us propose for the sake of illustration not only that they are pinned beneath ruins but they have also been pierced with some metal shards or splinters of wood found in the rubble. What then are those bodies likely to endure as they are

---

17. Gregory of Nyssa, *On the Soul and the Resurrection* (trans. Silvas), 213.
18. Gregory of Nyssa, *On the Soul and the Resurrection* (trans. Silvas), 213.

dragged from the ruins . . . ? They shall be discolored and torn and mangled in the most dire manner possible, the rubble and the nails lacerating them by the very force necessary to drag them out. It seems to me that some such experience also comes upon the soul when the divine power, for very love of man, drags its own from the ruins of the irrational and material.[19]

Through this vivid picture of the aftermath of a great city-leveling quake, an event all too common in Asia Minor, Macrina teaches that our state of disordered attachment is as destructive as the worst of quakes: it crushes, pins, and pierces us. God pulls us toward the freedom of holy detachment, the communion of blessedness; we suffer because we feel God's pull, but we cannot move toward God because we are embedded in, surrounded with, run through by our attachments. Macrina offers another analogy:

> If mud of a stickier sort is plastered thickly round a rope, and the end of the rope is put through a narrow opening, and someone pulls on it forcefully from the other side, then of course the rope obeys the one drawing it, while the mud plastered around it is scraped off during the forceful pulling and left outside the hole. Indeed, it is just because of this that the rope does not run easily through the passage, but has to endure a forceful tension from the one who pulls it. It seems to me that one can conceive of the soul in a similar way, as wrapped round by material and earthly attachments, toiling and being stretched as God attracts his own to himself, while the alien matter which has somehow sprung up with it is scraped off by force, which of course brings upon it keen and intolerable pains.[20]

If we are suffering, it means we are clinging to attachment to something; suffering is a reminder to let go more deeply, detach, take another step into surrender.

Macrina suffered when she discovered the tumor in her breast, but her hopes and fears were not what we might expect. She was not galvanized to action by a desire to avoid pain or death, nor did she reject treatment out of concerns about the piety of medicine. Rather, she was focused on doing God's will as she understood it and on surrendering all else.

---

19. Gregory of Nyssa, *On the Soul and the Resurrection* (trans. Silvas), 212–13.
20. Gregory of Nyssa, *On the Soul and the Resurrection* (trans. Silvas), 213.

Macrina experienced the will of God in her vocational calling. Her discernment was that subjecting herself to the medical care available in her day violated her vocational commitments. Nyssen put it this way: "she judged it worse than the affliction to lay bare any part of her body to the eye of a stranger."[21] This explanation appears, at first, perhaps even more puzzling than the choice it explains. We know that Macrina accepted the care of physicians in some instances—a physician was "seated beside her attending to her bodily condition"[22] during her last days. She seems to have had a high opinion of him for she used his work as an example of the defining characteristics of the soul. In his practice she saw the action of a "living and intellectual substance that infuses into an organic and sensate body the power of living and receiving the impressions of the senses."[23] Very possibly this doctor treated her without seeing any part of her body beyond her hands, face, and feet—she describes his ability to infer the state of her health from feeling her pulses and viewing the appearance of her complexion, the look of her eyes, and her position and posture. In contrast, medical treatment for breast cancer would have required baring her breast to a man, exposing herself not only to visual inspection but to extensive handling. A man, perhaps with male assistants also involved, would actually have to cut her open. Discomfort with this prospect is easy to understand—many Western women today struggle with the exposure and immodesty of breast cancer treatment—but the culture of ancient Cappadocia gave female modesty a weightier meaning. Modesty equated to female virtue, to reverence for God. Violation of modesty norms was not merely a matter of personal discomfort for the woman: an immodest woman was without virtue, she had stepped out of her place in the community, and such a woman was likely to face aggressive retribution, such as we saw in Thecla's story.

In her culture and time, Macrina's vocation was hard-won, and her place was held only through absolute commitment to virtue, made verifiable through the constant company of her mother. Separateness and modesty, to the point of hiddenness, defined her as a consecrated virgin. Although she tried to leave no ground for doubts or aspersions, the lives of the women at Annisa were still subject to gossip and insinuation as we saw in Basil's Letter 207 to the clergy of Neocaesaria (chapter 8) where he responds to

---

21. Gregory of Nyssa, *Life of Macrina* (trans. Silvas), 141.
22. Gregory of Nyssa, *Life of Macrina* (trans. Silvas), 179.
23. Gregory of Nyssa, *Life of Macrina* (trans. Silvas), 141.

rumors about the Annisa women, saying, "what Satan, the father of lies, has not undertaken to say up to this time, these audacious hearts and unbridled mouths are ever voicing unscrupulously."[24] The stakes were high for Macrina. The exposure of breast cancer treatment violated her vocational commitment to physical separateness and hiddenness and may also have undermined the reputation of her community. She turned to prayer:

> One evening, after waiting on her mother as usual with her own hand, [Macrina] passed within the sanctuary and fell prostrate before the God of all healings all night long and poured out a stream of water from her eyes upon the ground and used mud from the tears as a salve for the disease. But when her mother, in a thoroughly distressed state, again pleaded with her to put herself into the physician's hands, she declared it would be enough for the cure of the blight if her mother with her own hand applied the holy seal to the place.[25]

Macrina wore only one ornament, a necklace of slender chain that held an iron cross and an iron ring stamped with a cross. The ring contained a cavity in its band, and hidden in the cavity was a fragment of the true cross marked by the seal of the stamp of the cross. When Emmelia applied the holy seal to Macrina's tumor, she made the sign of the cross, and she may have applied the iron ring with its relic of the true cross inside.[26] Nyssen continues the story: "But when the mother put her hand within her bosom to apply the seal to the place, the seal was effective and the disease was no more."[27]

At her death Macrina's body bore only a "slight faint mark below the skin . . . like a scar made by a small needle."[28] Vetiana relates that this mark "appeared instead of the frightful tumor and remained right to the end as a memorial, I think, of the divine visitation."[29]

---

24. Basil of Caesaria, *Collection, Letter CCVII*, 579.
25. Gregory of Nyssa, *Life of Macrina* (trans. Silvas), 141.
26. Silvas, *Macrina the Younger*, footnote 125, 141.
27. Gregory of Nyssa, *Life of Macrina* (trans. Silvas), 141.
28. Gregory of Nyssa, *Life of Macrina* (trans. Silvas), 140.
29. Gregory of Nyssa, *Life of Macrina* (trans. Silvas), 142.

Meditation

Seat yourself comfortably and take a moment to focus and breathe. Invite stillness within and go over passages of your choice once to read the words, once to attend to your response, and again to hold the message in prayerful gaze.

If you are drawn to passages on suffering and surrender, consider Luke 22:41–44 and 54–71, Phil 2:8. Macrina said that when we are afflicted, "[God] is only claiming and drawing to himself whatever by his gift has come into generation."[30] Also: "it seems to me that one can conceive of the soul . . . as wrapped round by material and earthly attachments, toiling and being stretched as God attracts his own to himself, while the alien matter which has somehow sprung up with it is scraped off by force, which of course brings upon it keen and intolerable pains."[31] Consider your suffering. What are your attachments? Can you imagine releasing them? What would happen if you did?

If you are drawn to passages on healing, consider Ps 73:24–26, Mark 5:25–34, Jas 5:16.

---

30. Gregory of Nyssa, *On the Soul and the Resurrection* (trans. Silvas), 213.
31. Gregory of Nyssa, *On the Soul and the Resurrection (Trans. Silvas)*, 213.

10

Famine, Justice, and Holy Detachment

"I was hungry and you gave me food, I was thirsty and you gave me something to drink, I was a stranger and you welcomed me, naked and you gave me clothing, sick and you took care of me." (Matt 25:35–36)

ANNISA WAS NOT ONLY a retreat but also a working farm. In good years, the winters of central Anatolia brought snow and rain. Spring found the earth moist under the plow, and sunny days alternated with showers, creating a climate perfect for germinating seeds and nursing seedlings. Summers were hot, but there was usually some rain, and the rivers running with snowmelt could be used to irrigate. There were many years when harvests exceeded demand and livestock thrived and multiplied.

The agricultural bounty of Anatolia was managed within a complex socioeconomic hierarchy. The ordinary people worked the land, minded the herds, and labored to transform raw materials, like grain and wool, into end-products such as bread and clothing. Local aristocrats owned the land and either owned these laborers as slaves or paid them a small portion of the produce of their labor as a wage.

As the new capital city of Constantinople was built and populated, the empire placed enormous demands on the region. Resource extraction was accomplished through a highly organized, and often corrupt, system. The emperor tasked his governors with delivering the wealth of their provinces to the imperial treasury (after retaining a share). The governors gave bureaucrats authority to collect payment in goods and services from the local landed gentry (while skimming off what they could), and the gentry delivered up the produce of the laborers on their lands (after keeping what they deemed necessary for themselves). The predictable result was that the people at the bottom of the hierarchy were affected the most severely. The marginal grew poor, the poor grew poorer.

While the "working poor" of the ancient agricultural economy struggled to hold their own, Anatolia, situated on the eastern edge of the Roman Empire, also received refugees and exiles from neighboring areas. People displaced from their lands by wars, or by unopposed invasions, traveled through the region in search of food, shelter, safety, and work. Nyssen, in the first in his series of sermons, "On the Love of the Poor," describes these refugees:

> We have seen in these days a great number of the naked and homeless. For the most part they are victims of war who knock at our doors. But there is also no lack of strangers and exiles, and their hands, stretched and imploring, can be seen everywhere. Their roof is the sky. For shelter they use porticos, alleys, and deserted corners of the town. They hide in the cracks of walls like owls. Their clothing consists of wretched rags... Their cup is the hollow of their hand, their storeroom their pocket, or rather whatever part of it has not been torn and cannot hold whatever is put into it. For a dining table they use their joined knees, and their lamp is the sun...[1]

Nyssen speaks on the injustice of the discrepancy between rich and poor and on the terrible and utter destitution of anyone so unfortunate as to suffer from a chronic illness or physical disability. He contrasts the lives of the poor with the those of the rich:

> [They] squander their goods on enormous houses and superfluous ornaments. They also like to rest on magnificent beds covered with flowery hangings, richly embroidered. They have massively expensive silver tables made for them; some are remarkable in the sheen of the metal; on others an artist engraves scenes and one is thus able, during the meal, to delight in beautiful legends. Think further of the wine bowls, tripods, jars, ewers, platters, all sorts of cups; the clowns, mimes, kithara-players, chanters, poets, male

1. Holman, *Hungry Are Dying*, 194.

and female musicians, dancers, and all the equipment of debauchery, boys with effeminate coiffures, shameless girls . . .

While all this is going on in the house, a myriad of Lazaruses sit at the gate, some dragging themselves along painfully . . . They cry and are not heard over the flutes' whistling, loud songs, and the cackling of bawling laughter . . .[2]

Some people, doubtless, were moved by Nyssen's urging and gave more to the poor. Most of the privileged, however, continued just as they had before, turning a blind eye to the insecurity growing around them as every resource was overworked and overused. In particular, they ignored one very important element of economic security in Anatolia, namely local access to emergency food supplies.

Every farmer knows that there will be poor years. In a year of meager harvests, towns in other areas, along coasts and big rivers, could bring in shiploads of grain to feed the people, but on the mountain-girded, landlocked plateaus of Cappadocia and Pontus, there was no such option. Imported grain would have to be packed or pulled over mountain passes. Relief deliveries would be small, slow, and expensive. The people of the region traditionally looked after themselves by planning ahead, stockpiling surplus grain from good years against the inevitable hard years when weather, disease, or pests would destroy their crops. However, under the pressure to build the new capital and keep the rich and powerful of the empire supplied, farmers were left with no grain to put aside. This meant that they had nothing to fall back on when, in about 368 to 370 CE, Anatolia suffered a severe drought, leading to crop failures, widespread hardship, and severe hunger. Basil described the situation in a homily:

> We see how the heavens have grown hard and unyielding, naked and bereft of clouds, while the clear blue sky makes an unwelcome and distressing appearance. In the past, we used to long for even a glimpse of the sky when it remained covered with clouds for long intervals, leaving us in darkness and shadow. The earth is completely dried up, terrible to see, barren and utterly unsuitable for planting. Its surface is cracked and broken up by the unrelenting glare of the sun. Abundant and reliable springs have failed us, and the flow of the great rivers have dried up; tiny children now play within their banks, while women carry

---

2. Holman, *Hungry Are Dying*, 198.

> burdens across them easily. Many have nothing to drink and are in danger of perishing from thirst . . .[3]
>
> Some of the seeds dried up without germinating, buried by the plow beneath clumps of dried earth. The rest, after just beginning to take root and sprout, were withered by the hot wind in a manner pitiful to see . . . Farmers sit in their fields . . . weeping for their wasted efforts. They look at their young children and burst into tears, they see their wives and wail with grief . . .[4]

Families walked away from their homes, lands, and villages in search of food. Having little or nothing that could be sold or traded for a meal, people bartered the clothes off their backs to feed their families. Basil commented, "Our sheep give birth to many lambs, yet there are more people who go about naked than there are shorn sheep."[5] Hungry people begged at the gates of the wealthy. Some were driven even to the extreme of cannibalism, so complete was their desperation and misery. Many died slow, horrible starvation deaths.

Amid this terrible suffering, the wealthy of the region ate well and held back storehouses filled with grain, driving prices higher and increasing their profits instead of feeding the hungry and dying people around them. Basil preached forcefully against this appalling injustice and exhorted the rich to take prompt, generous, and compassionate action:

> Hunger is the most severe of human maladies, the very worst kind of death [Basil goes on to give a detailed and graphic description of death by starvation]. How many torments does the one who neglects such a [starving] body deserve? What extreme cruelty does such a person not surpass? . . . Whoever has the ability to remedy the suffering of others, but chooses rather to withhold aid out of selfish motives, may be properly judged the equivalent of a murderer.[6]
>
> Let those who account greed a virtue and amass far more wealth than they actually need demonstrate now the value of the things they have treasured up.[7]

---

3. Basil of Caesarea, *In Time of Famine and Drought*, 50.
4. Basil of Caesarea, *In Time of Famine and Drought*, 51.
5. Basil of Caesarea, *In Time of Famine and Drought*, 52.
6. Basil of Caesarea, *In Time of Famine and Drought*, 58.
7. Basil of Caesarea, *In Time of Famine and Drought*, 53.

> The times are calling you to return to the mother of the commandments. Take exceeding care, lest the opportunity of celebration and reward pass you by . . . take hold of the commandment and discharge it before the opportunity flees away . . . give but a little, and you will gain much.[8]

Meanwhile at Annisa, Macrina and Peter used their grain stores to feed the hungry so that "crowds from all sides poured into the retreat where they lived, drawn by the report of their generosity."[9] They were able to provide such an abundance of food that the dry farm land around the retreat "seemed to be a city, so great was the throng of visitors."[10] In describing Macrina's miracles and wonderful works, Nyssen refers to her "incredible husbandry during the famine, when the grain was being dispensed for the relief of need, and yet gave no sign of diminishment."[11]

Macrina's community also took in orphans, and during the famine there were many—children whose parents had died, those abandoned on roadsides by parents who could not feed them, and those left at the gates of the estate by parents hoping their little ones would be saved. Emmelia's feelings toward these children would have been shaped by her own beginnings as an orphan, taken in and nurtured by adults who were struggling to survive the terrible hardships of the Great Persecution. Macrina was committed to caring for these children, and Basil strongly promoted caring for orphans in monastic communities. They set about taking in all the children brought to the gates and found on the nearby roads.

This good work raised a whole range of practical challenges. Annisa was a community of adults who strove for constant and undistracted attention to prayer. Integrating numbers of undernourished, ill, and traumatized infants and children in this setting required adjustments, and the leaders would have faced a steep learning curve in the early days. Glimpses into the lessons they learned can be inferred from the instructions for monastic communities that Basil added to his rule as he expanded the Small Asketikon into the Long Rules. In his rule, Basil aspired to nothing less than setting down a written key through which a collection of people, with all the flaws of our common nature, might embody the gospel in shared life. In Long Rule 15, he describes how monastic communities should enroll

---

8. Basil of Caesarea, *In Time of Famine and Drought*, 58.
9. Gregory of Nyssa, *Life of Macrina* (trans. Silvas), 124.
10. Gregory of Nyssa, *Life of Macrina* (trans. Silvas), 124.
11. Gregory of Nyssa, *Life of Macrina* (trans. Silvas), 148.

children and provide for their care and formation. While his ideas reflect his culture and time in history, he addresses human foibles and failings that are all too familiar even today.

The earliest experiments in bringing children into the community must have placed the children in living quarters alongside adult monastics. Advice on separating the living quarters for children and adults is an important focus for Basil, and he argues that this is critical in solving a number of problems. Children's attitudes toward adults became one area of concern. We sometimes hear older people complain that children "these days" are not as respectful, dutiful, and obedient as they used to be, "in my day we respected our elders!" Basil's instructions in the Long Rules suggest that, even in the fourth century, kids did not always show the deference and courtesy adults preferred. One advantage of separate living quarters, he advised, would be that greater "rarity of association" would lead children to "reverence" adults.

Also familiar to us in present times, it seems that adults in the fourth century did not always behave in ways that really merited this reverence. One concern was that adults might lead children into misdeeds through the example of their own faults. Basil argued that keeping adults and children separate was important because "if at any time these [adults] should happen to be off their guard"[12] and behave badly, they would not influence the children for the worse. Likewise, he hoped that limited contact with adults would keep children from witnessing "their elders repeatedly delinquent in that which they themselves do aright."[13] Besides undoing progress toward good behavior, Basil was concerned that children might develop a smug and conceited attitude as a result of watching adults struggle and fall short. His instructions also reflect prudent caution about preventing more serious problems in adult behavior when he advises that housing adults and children separately will prevent the development of "precocious and unbecoming" behavior in children, inspired by "close association with older persons."[14]

Of course, keeping children in their own lodgings also solved the problem of children disrupting adult activities and shielded adults at prayer

---

12. Basil of Caesarea, *Complete Works*, Long Rules 15, loc 14982.
13. Basil of Caesarea, *Complete Works*, Long Rules 15, loc 14982.
14. Basil of Caesarea, *Complete Works*, Long Rules 15, loc 14982.

from the distraction and annoyance of overhearing the "drilling which is necessary for the young in learning their lessons."[15]

Basil goes on to advise that a mature person with "more than average experience and who has a reputation for patience"[16] be put in charge of the little ones. This person was to form and lead the young through consistent good example and wise instruction, teaching the maxims of the book of Proverbs (as Emmelia had done with Macrina and Basil himself) and historical accounts of admirable lives. The teacher was to hold out rewards "for memorizing names and facts. In this way, joyfully and with a relaxed mind, [the children] will achieve their aim without pain . . ."[17] When the youngsters needed correction, the teacher was to guide them with "fatherly kindness, applying remedies proper to each fault, so that, while the penalty for the fault is being exacted, the soul may be exercised in interior tranquility."[18] Basil discusses fitting "remedies" for anger, eating outside of permitted times, eating immoderately or "in an unseemly fashion," telling lies, insulting others, and spreading rumors.

While Basil himself had little, if any, experience living with or supervising children, Macrina could well have been his prototype for the ideal instructor—mature (around forty at the time), experienced with children, patient, and able to inspire not only great achievement but also great respect and affection. Eight years later, when Macrina died, Nyssen described the "vehement . . . grief of those who had called her their mother and nurse. These were the ones whom she had rescued when they had been exposed by the roadside at the time of the famine."[19] Silvas suggests that the content of Long Rule 15 was developed during visits to Annisa in the period of the famine. Could it be seen as a work of mutual effort and contribution, in which Macrina provided the working model and material of discussion, while Basil articulated in formal terms what she was doing?

Macrina cared for the children and adults of her community, with all their needs and foibles, while she also led and instructed them in responding, in work and prayer, to the awful challenges of the famine. During this time, she probably shared her teachings on the rich man and Lazarus, the parable we reviewed in chapter 9, which Nyssen references in his comment

---

15. Basil of Caesarea, *Complete Works, Long Rules 15*, loc 14982.
16. Basil of Caesarea, *Complete Works, Long Rules 15*, loc 14994.
17. Basil of Caesarea, *Complete Works, Long Rules 15*, loc 15005.
18. Basil of Caesarea, *Complete Works, Long Rules 15*, loc 14995.
19. Gregory of Nyssa, *Life of Macrina* (trans. Silvas), 137.

about myriad Lazaruses, and which speaks directly to the injustice underlying the mass hunger in Cappadocia.

Macrina began her instruction on this parable by laying some ground work for interpretation. She argued that the story should not be interpreted literally but understood through a "more subtle contemplation."[20] Although told in bodily terms, she points out, it is a story about souls of the dead. "Inasmuch as the bodies of [the rich man and Lazarus] are in the tomb and their souls are not in the body,"[21] she asks, how can the rich man feel any flame? What kind of tongue could he wish to cool with drops of water? What sort of finger could Lazarus use to sprinkle him? And Abraham's bosom, what is that? Literal reading is confusing and, on close examination, a bit absurd.

Likewise, Macrina holds that Hades is not a physical location: "It seems to me that whether in the pagan or in the divine writings, this word for a place in which souls are said to be signifies nothing else but a transition to the non-apparent and invisible world."[22] Hades is a state of being, not a geographic place. Likewise, she instructed, the gulf dividing the rich man from Lazarus and Abraham is not, "a rift in the earth, but is made up of those decisions during this life"[23] that make our souls either more faithful mirrors imaging the divine or less faithful in holding that image (see Appendix 1).

The Greek word used in Scripture for "bosom" referred to the lap or bosom of a person and was also used to describe a bay or cove of the sea. Building from this, Macrina says, "Just as in applied usage we call a certain embrasure of the sea a 'bosom,' so the Word seems to me to convey the sense of that immeasurable good above by the term 'bosom,' in that all who sail through this life with virtue, when they set out from here, moor their souls in that 'bosom' of the good, as in a waveless harbor."[24] She described the experienced flames of Hades as "the privation of good now manifest to them [which] became a flame smoldering in the soul, so that it craves but does not obtain the consolation of one drop of that sea of the good engulfing the holy"[25] (see Appendix 1).

---

20. Gregory of Nyssa, *On the Soul and the Resurrection* (trans. Silvas), 203.
21. Gregory of Nyssa, *On the Soul and the Resurrection* (trans. Silvas), 204.
22. Gregory of Nyssa, *On the Soul and the Resurrection* (trans. Silvas), 197–98.
23. Gregory of Nyssa, *On the Soul and the Resurrection* (trans. Silvas), 205.
24. Gregory of Nyssa, *On the Soul and the Resurrection* (trans. Silvas), 205.
25. Gregory of Nyssa, *On the Soul and the Resurrection* (trans. Silvas), 205.

FAMINE, JUSTICE, AND HOLY DETACHMENT

Macrina interpreted the parable of Lazarus and the rich man as practical wisdom that applied quite directly to the problems in Cappadocia at that time. That is, the devastation and suffering throughout the countryside were caused not so much by the drought, bad though it was, as by humans placing greed and self-serving desire above the love of one another. The rich, in their passion to indulge themselves more lavishly, chose to withhold storehouses full of grain while the poor died of starvation. Unbridled human appetites, desires, and urges were playing out on a large scale, causing devastation. Macrina used Jesus' teaching story to help her community learn from these terrible events, grow in wisdom, and progress on the path of theosis. I offer here an interpretation of the instruction she might have given to the people at Annisa:

Macrina's Wisdom on Holy Detachment

In this time of hardship, we see great suffering caused by the choices of people who are trying to serve themselves even as they harm their neighbors. These people are blinded by appetite, desire, fear, and anger, and yet these human drives and emotions are not forces of evil in themselves. Indeed, appetites hold within them instincts useful to bodily life, and great energies are generated by desire, anger, and fear. Like the fire of the blacksmith, these drives and emotions can be used to shape tools for the soul's work, or to hammer out chains that bind us in slavery, or to harden the weapons of domination and war. The difference depends on how we order our choices.

If we mistake self-gratification for the joy and freedom of divine communion, we live our lives serving idols, chasing after empty objects and meaningless missions that we put in the place of God. In this case, our appetite, desire, fear, and anger excite passionate attachment to delusions: we seek fulfillment through such things as sensory pleasure, fame, achievement, wealth, and power over other people. When the momentary satisfaction and self-enhancement of one such prize fades, we seek another, and then more, leading only to hunger for still more. Soon we become the servants of our compulsive need for ever greater indulgence.

As we labor and grasp after these things, a gulf widens, separating us from our true selves. Desire does not mature toward beauty but leads us into lives of self-indulgence, addiction, exploitation, and self-importance. Anger feeds rivalry, conflict, and alienation from other people. Fear becomes cowardice. To gain what we feel we must have, we cut corners when it comes to doing what is right. We take more than we can use even when others have less than they require. We tell small lies, and bigger ones, we tell ourselves that our own injustice is really justified. In such ways, by our choices, we separate ourselves from the good—from justice, truth, love, humility, courage, generosity, temperance, patience—from the very freedom and beauty in which we were created.

Such disordered and mistaken passions can hold us in thrall for a whole lifetime. We may even tell ourselves that it does not matter whether we try to choose the good—we are, after all, going to die anyway. But the truth is that a life of mistaken and disordered attachment will leave us, when the time comes to cross over into the disembodied state, cut off, divided from the beloved and from our own true, essential nature.

Like the rich man in the parable of Lazarus, a person whose life is given over to specious and idolatrous attachments will die only to face another death. That is, as he leaves the embodied state, such a person will see the truth of his life, recognize the delusions he has chased, and burn with thirst for the good. He is overwhelmed with longing. Regret and shame drive him back toward the life now left behind, desperate to make amends, or at least to save others from making the same mistakes, but there is no way back.

Even for such a person, there is still the promise of the resurrection, still the hope of healing in the hereafter through the fires of purification. But if we have prepared well in life, death can lead easily and freely into the illimitable good of the divine embrace. In that case, like Lazarus who, having surrendered, is gathered in the bosom of Abraham, we will be home. Our every need will be met and every hope fulfilled because God will be all in all to us—our house, our food and drink, our light, our riches, and every imaginable kind of good to sustain our souls (see Appendix 1). Those who participate in the divine good are filled with blessings, and as "the fountain of the good wells up unfailingly (cf. John 4:14),"[26] the partaker grows in capacity to contain the abundance of the good. Like Lazarus, we can die without being torn by the need to correct or undo the embodied lives we leave behind. We can be truly free.

Surrender can open us to be filled with blessings even while we are in this embodied life. When we can release disordered attachments, there is nothing to hinder us from drinking deeply and being filled with the beauty and the blessings of the present. In

---

26. Gregory of Nyssa, *On the Soul and the Resurrection* (trans. Silvas), 217.

the freedom of holy detachment, our emotions and appetites fall into line according to our true, created nature. We become united within ourselves so that we are filled, saturated with good in doing what we know to be good. In this state, everything within draws us into blessing. Our thirst can be quenched and our hunger sated, truly, sweetly, deeply, and completely. The potency of this enjoyment renders compulsive desires stale.

In this way, detachment allows the soul to return to itself accurately. So unified, the soul can hold up a clear and undistorted face to mirror its archetype. This is the way of theosis—we take on likeness to the divine as we reflect in our beings, feelings, choices, and actions—in small measure, scaled to our own capacity—the transcendent good of divine nature.

Macrina's instruction turns us toward the practical, applied wisdom of detachment. This central principle of ascetic practice was articulated by the Mahavira almost nine hundred years before Macrina's lifetime, as we saw in chapter 2. Often called non-attachment, it is central not only in the Christian tradition but in Buddhism, Taoism, Hinduism, Baháʼí Faith, and schools of philosophy such as stoicism. In Macrina's teaching, detachment is the antidote to the passions that lead to social injustice, the basis of virtue, and foundation of the gospel life which is, of course, love. The love, that is, that Jesus spoke of when he said, "I give you a new commandment, that you love one another. Just as I have loved you, you also should love one another" (John 13:34).

Meditation

Consider 1 John 3:16–18, Matt 25:34–46, the parable of Lazarus and the rich man (Luke 16:19–31), and Macrina's wisdom:

> In the freedom of detachment, our emotions and appetites fall into line according to our true, created nature. We become united within ourselves so that we are filled, saturated with good in doing what we know to be good. In this state, everything within draws us into blessing. Our thirst can be quenched and our hunger sated, truly, sweetly, deeply, and completely. The potency of this enjoyment renders compulsive desires stale.
>
> Detachment allows the soul to return to itself accurately. So unified, the soul can hold up its own clear and undistorted face to mirror its archetype. This is the way of theosis—we take on likeness to the divine as we reflect in our beings, feelings, choices,

and actions—in small measure, scaled to our own capacity—the transcendent good of divine nature.

Seat yourself comfortably and take a moment to focus and breathe. Invite stillness within. Read your passages once with attention to the words, once listening to your response, and again holding the message in prayerful gaze.

11

Like an Incense Offering: The Grace of a Happy Death

"Where, O death, is your victory? Where, O death, is your sting?" (1 Cor 15:55)

THE YEARS AROUND THE famine were marked by great changes in Macrina's family. Basil was elected bishop around 370. The following winter, mother Emmelia came to the end of her long, well-lived, and fulfilled life. She was between sixty and sixty-five, which Nyssen describes as a ripe old age. On her death bed, she spoke words of blessing for all her children, and she passed to God in the arms of Peter and Macrina. Nyssen describes the scene:

> As these two sat by her on each side of the bed, she took each of them by the hand, and spoke to God in these her last words. "To you, O Lord, I dedicate my first fruits and the tithe of my pangs. For this my first-born is the first fruits (Exodus 13:2), and this, my last labour, is the tenth (Numbers 18:21). They are both consecrated to you by the Law and are your votive offerings..."
> ... And when she had ceased her blessing, she ceased her life, having bidden her children to lay her body in their father's tomb. They fulfilled her charge and gave themselves to philosophy with still loftier resolve, always striving with their own life and eclipsing their earlier achievement with others that followed.[1]

---

1. Gregory of Nyssa, *Life of Macrina* (trans. Silvas), 124.

Soon after Emmelia's death, Basil ordained Peter to the priesthood. For the first time, Annisa had a resident priest. The community became more defined as a monastery with Peter presiding as male priest-monk superior, head of the whole community with its separate houses of men, women, and children, while Macrina continued as female superior. Meanwhile, in 372 Basil consecrated Nyssen as bishop of Nyssa.

For the next eight years, Basil presided as metropolitan bishop, Gregory as bishop of Nyssa, Peter as head of the home monastery, and Macrina as foundress, teacher, and leader. The family continued to live, teach, and preach their Nicene Christianity while controversy and power struggles raged on in the church and empire under Emperor Valens. The show-down between Basil and Valens (chapter 8) took place during this time, and Nyssen was the target of such hostilities that he could not come to his home province, and so could not visit Annisa, for the entire eight years: "I was everywhere hounded out of my own fatherland by the leaders of heresy."[2]

In August 378, Emperor Valens was killed in battle, and then, perhaps in September or October that same year,[3] around the age of forty-nine, Basil passed over into disembodied life. Although he suffered with chronic illness, Basil's death seems to have been unexpected. He did not go home to die in the peace of his retreat or the arms of family but passed to God far from Annisa. His friend Nazianzen, who wrote a dozen epigrams in his honor, commented, "such was the will of Christ that he might join thee early."[4] Both Nazianzen and Nyssen were struck by the abrupt silencing of Basil's voice. Nazianzen lamented: "He is gone, the herald, the bond of glorious peace is gone . . . Basil, the deep voiced messenger of truth, the Christians' bright eye, shining with all the beauty of the soul . . . Alas the lips of Basil are closed and silent."[5] Describing his grief after Basil's passing, Nyssen said, "we see one who was so lately alive and vocal becoming all of a sudden bereft of breath and voice and movement, with all the natural faculties of sense extinguished."[6] Macrina received the news of Basil's passing by messenger, and grief hit hard:

> She suffered in soul at so great a privation . . . as they say, the proving of gold takes place in several crucibles, such that if some

2. Gregory of Nyssa, *Life of Macrina* (trans. Silvas), 126.
3. Sylvas, *Macrina the Younger*, 125fn68.
4. Henderson, *Greek Anthology Books 7–8*, VIII:9, 405.
5. Henderson, *Greek Anthology Books 7–8*, VIII:3–5, 402–3.
6. Gregory of Nyssa, *On the Soul and the Resurrection* (trans. Silvas), 172.

impurity escapes the first smelting, it is separated out in the second, and again, till in the last one, all admixture of dross is purged away from the matter, so that the most accurate test of proven gold is that when it has passed through every smelting it casts off no more dross.

It was something like this that took place in her. When her lofty cast of mind had been tested by the varied assaults of grief, the unadulterated and undebased quality of her soul was revealed on every side—firstly by the departure of her brother [Naucratius], then after this by the parting from her mother, and thirdly when Basil, the common glory of the family, was removed from human life. Yet she continued firm, like an unconquerable athlete, not buckling at any stage before the assaults of misfortune.[7]

The grieving Nyssen also continued firmly and tirelessly in his episcopal labors. In 379, about seven months after Basil's death, he attended the Council of Antioch. This was a landmark event in which bishops from both the eastern and western Roman Empire came together. At the council, Nyssen carried Basil's cause forward, arguing for the co-equal Trinity, the orthodox Nicene faith. The assembly was able to reach agreement at least to the degree of approving the Synodal Letter of Damasus, which affirmed the Nicene Creed over the various competing and alternative interpretations of the Trinity.

Having thus seen Basil's great work through to a major victory, Nyssen's thoughts turned toward home and the family he had not been able to visit for eight years. He especially wanted to see Macrina, "who was for me in place of a mother and a teacher and every good."[8] In June 379[9] he set out: "I went to her then with haste, to share with her the calamity of our brother. Indeed my soul was keening at so exceedingly painful a loss, and I sought one with whom I might share my tears, one who bore the same burden of grief."[10]

Constantine's road through Cappadocia, cut in the early fourth century to supply the grand new capitol at Constantinople, covered the three hundred miles or so between Antioch to Annisa, crossing mountains and traversing rugged terrain. By horse or camel, the trip would have taken at least two weeks, but more often it was probably a sojourn of a month or

---

7. Gregory of Nyssa, *Life of Macrina* (trans. Silvas), 125.
8. Gregory of Nyssa, *Letter Nineteen*, 89.
9. Sylvas, *Macrina the Younger*, 126fn69, 70, 73.
10. Gregory of Nyssa, *On the Soul and the Resurrection* (trans. Silvas), 171.

two, with stops to visit, rest, and conduct business along the way. In Letter Nineteen, translated by Silvas, Nyssen refers to such a stop on his journey home: "I had halted among the Cappadocians, when unexpectedly I received some disturbing news of her [Macrina]. There was a ten day's journey between us, so I covered the whole distance as quickly as possible and at last reached Pontus."[11]

When he was about a day away from Annisa, Nyssen experienced a dream-vision in which he was holding the relics of martyrs in his hands. The relics carried the very essence of Macrina's vision and teaching: "A radiance shone out from them like that which comes from a pure mirror when it is turned to face the sun, so that my eyes were dazzled by the brilliance of the rays."[12] He woke, wondered at the meaning of this vision, and fell back into sleep. The vision came to him a second time in the same way, and then once more before the night was over.

The next day, as he crossed over the Iris River at the edge of the estate, about five miles from the dwellings, he stopped to speak with attendants on lookout there. They told him that Peter had set out to meet him four days before, going a different way, and that Macrina was in a very weak condition. Nyssen rushed on to reach her side.

As he and his traveling party came up to the monastery buildings, the men poured out from their quarters and hurried to greet them. The women gathered at the entrance of the church and waited there to share greetings and prayers and to receive blessing, "which they accepted with one gracious bow of the head, turned back, and withdrew to their own quarters."[13] Macrina was not among them. Nyssen narrates:

> Someone led me to the house where the great one was and opened the door, and I entered within that sacred abode. Though she was already greatly incapacitated by weakness, she was not lying on a bed or couch, but on the floor, on a board strewn with sacking, with another board propping up her head by supporting the sinew of the neck at a slant and supporting her neck comfortably.[14]

When she saw her little brother bishop in the doorway, Macrina raised up on her elbow. She was too weak to stand, but she placed her hands on the floor and leaned out from her pallet, coming as near to

---

11. Gregory of Nyssa, *Letter Nineteen*, 88.
12. Gregory of Nyssa, *Life of Macrina* (trans. Silvas), 126.
13. Gregory of Nyssa, *Life of Macrina* (trans. Silvas), 127.
14. Gregory of Nyssa, *Life of Macrina* (trans. Silvas), 128.

him as she could. He ran to her, took her head in his hands, bowed to the ground, then raised her up again and settled her back on her resting place. Macrina raised her hands up to God, saying "Yes! Even this favour you have granted me, O God, and have not deprived me of my desire . . . !"[15] (Exclamation points added.)

Brother and sister talked together for the first time in eight years and one of the last times in life. When they spoke of Basil's passing, Nyssen was flooded with grief: "my soul drooped, my face fell dejected, and the tears streamed from my eyes."[16] Gently, Macrina reminded him that faith teaches us that we need not grieve for those who have passed on to live with God. Grief is "the passion only of those who have no hope (1 Thess 4:13)."[17] She asked him, "what exactly is it about death in itself that seems especially grievous to you?"[18] Gregory responded, speaking of the shock and pain of witnessing death,

> [When] the principle of life, whatever it may be, vanishes all at once and is no longer evident, just as a lamp is extinguished when the flame, which only a moment before was alight, neither remains in the wick nor passes to some other place but vanishes entirely. How then can such a change be borne without grief by one who has nothing evident to rely on any more? For we hear the exodus of the soul, and we see what is left. But what it was that has been removed we do not know, neither what its nature is nor whither it has gone. For neither earth, nor air, nor water, nor any other of the elements shows this force that has quit the body, at the withdrawal of which there remains only a corpse already set for corruption.[19]

Macrina, though too ill to rise, responded to his grief by talking with him at length about the nature of human life and death, the soul, and the journey of faith. "She explained everything clearly and in sequence as one inspired by the power of the Holy Spirit. Her speech flowed with complete ease like water streaming downhill from a fountain unimpeded."[20] Nyssen tried to describe the spiritual strength that allowed her to share and teach even as she lay dying: "Fever was consuming her vital force and impelling

---

15. Gregory of Nyssa, *Life of Macrina* (trans. Silvas), 128.
16. Gregory of Nyssa, *Life of Macrina* (trans. Silvas), 128.
17. Gregory of Nyssa, *On the Soul and the Resurrection* (trans. Silvas), 172.
18. Gregory of Nyssa, *On the Soul and the Resurrection* (trans. Silvas), 172.
19. Gregory of Nyssa, *On the Soul and the Resurrection* (trans. Silvas), 172–173.
20. Gregory of Nyssa, *Life of Macrina* (trans. Silvas), 129.

her towards death, yet she refreshed her body as with some kind of dew, and so kept her mind unimpaired in the contemplation of higher things."[21] The conversation had such deep impact on Nyssen that he later transcribed it in its entirety, giving us *On the Soul and the Resurrection*. An interpretation of some of Macrina's wisdom for her brother is offered here.

Macrina's Wisdom on Life and Death

We know from our faith that our souls are eternal and God has given us the great hope of the resurrection. Even so, darkness and pain can lead to doubt, and within this doubt there is even the fear that there is no God, no soul—the fear that death is the end of all being.

In fear, we grasp for proof of God and the soul, hard evidence that the things we cannot see are real. Maybe we examine the elements or study natural science in search of definite answers. In the end, however, this does not help because natural science allows us to learn only about those things we can detect with our sense organs and interact with as substances. Limiting our contemplation of what is to these things is like shielding ourselves within a hut where we cannot see the wonders of the heavens, not because they are not there but because we are blinded by the walls and the roof we have built.

No one can prove God or the soul, and no one can explain how the resurrection will work. If we demand tangible proofs and mechanical explanations of these great mysteries, we achieve nothing except to confine ourselves in our huts where we cannot see the sky. There can be a certain comfort in this—at least we feel secure in being able to describe, define, and analyze what is before us—but in the end we are cut off from the very basis of hope.

We can, when we are ready, step out onto the ground of faith, into the embrace of the limitless heavens. Here we cannot doubt that the universe is greater than what we can sense and analyze. The vastness of all being is before us; we behold unknowns beyond unknowns; we may even experience, in a real way, the infinite presence beyond our proofs and reasonings. Here we can gaze upon the great mystery of being and listen for the truths it holds out to us. "By faith we understand that the worlds were prepared by the Word of God, so that what is seen was made from things that are not visible" (Heb 11:3).

---

21. Gregory of Nyssa, *Life of Macrina* (trans. Silvas), 129.

> The ineffable wisdom of God is so manifest in the universe that, once we come out of our huts, we are constantly assured and reassured of the divine all around us, of the very energy and motion that is holding everything in existence from moment to moment.
>
> Likewise, the soul so organizes and animates the substances that make up our bodies, so permeates them with the presence and energy and motion of life, that we are constantly assured and reassured that we are beings—that spirit is in us, creating us and sustaining us in some way beyond our comprehension. This is only more evident when the spirit passes out of the body and what is before us is no longer the person we knew but only the lifeless elements of the flesh. In this moment, the soul is freed, given back to its original, divinely formed nature.
>
> Those who die in bondage to vice must be healed in the hereafter through purifying fire. For a person purified in life, death opens into unity with the true, divinely created self. From there, the only thing left is love. The only thing left is to be absorbed in, and filled with, blessing.

When their conversation was complete, Macrina begged Nyssen to rest after his long journey. He thirsted for more time in her presence, but at her urging he went out to the garden and lay in the shade of an arbor covered with trailing vines. The lovely setting gave him little joy, for he was in turmoil. He saw the meaning of his vision the night before—the relics in the dream were her remains, dead though still shining with the "indwelling grace of the Spirit."[22] Nyssen was washed over in grief. He stayed there in the garden in heavy sadness. Macrina, as if aware of his despondency, sent him a message to take heart: she was feeling better. This was not said to deceive, Nyssen explains, but was true in a way he did not understand until later. Her revival was like:

> . . . a runner who has passed his adversary and already draws near to the end of the stadium, when he draws near the prize and sees the victor's crown, rejoices inwardly . . . and calls out his victory to his supporters among the spectators. It was in such a frame of mind that she, too, told us to cherish more favourable hopes for her, for she was already looking to the prize of the upward call (Philippians 3:14) and all but uttering the apostle's words for

---

22. Gregory of Nyssa, *Life of Macrina* (trans. Silvas), 129.

herself... I have fought the good fight, I have finished the course, I have kept the faith (II Timothy 4:7)[23]

With spirits raised by her encouraging words, Nyssen and his party enjoyed the hospitality of Macrina's house. Various good things were put before them, giving them much pleasure "since the attentiveness of the great one extended even to such trifles as these."[24] Later she called him back and they talked again. This time she reviewed the stories of their family and of her life, giving thanks to God for the blessings they had all received, and she spoke to Nyssen of his work and ministry. He was nourished and moved by her words:

> I was wishing it were possible to extend the length of the day so that she might not cease to delight our ears. But the voice of the psalm-singers was summoning us to the thanksgiving at the lighting of the lamps, and the great one, having sent me off to church, withdrew once more to God in prayers, and in these she spent the night.[25]

The next morning, Nyssen saw that Macrina had reached the "uttermost limit of her life."[26] Fever had drained her strength, but even so she offered him comfort: "seeing our weakness of mind, she tried to divert us from our gloomy forebodings, and once again dispersed our grief of soul with those beautiful words of hers, though from now on she did so with short and labored breathing."[27] In the next hours, Nyssen was both torn and inspired as he witnessed, on the one hand, a person dying, and on the other a soul at peace and living fully:

> For not even during her last breaths did she suffer any qualm at the prospect of her departure, or flinch at her separation from this life... All this seemed to me to be no longer of the human order. It was as if by some dispensation an angel had assumed human form, with whom, not having any kinship or affinity with the life of the flesh, it was not at all unreasonable that the mind should remain in an unperturbed state, since the flesh did not drag it down to its own passions. Accordingly it seemed to me that she was then making manifest to those present that divine

23. Gregory of Nyssa, *Life of Macrina* (trans. Silvas), 130.
24. Gregory of Nyssa, *Life of Macrina* (trans. Silvas), 130.
25. Gregory of Nyssa, *Life of Macrina* (trans. Silvas), 132.
26. Gregory of Nyssa, *Life of Macrina* (trans. Silvas), 132.
27. Gregory of Nyssa, *Life of Macrina* (trans. Silvas), 132.

LIKE AN INCENSE OFFERING: THE GRACE OF A HAPPY DEATH

and pure love of the unseen Bridegroom . . . for in truth, her race was towards her Beloved, and no other of the pleasures of this life diverted her eye to itself.[28]

The day passed in this way, and as evening came, Macrina seemed to perceive beauty before her and to grow more eager. Her pallet was turned to face the east. Gazing toward the heavens, gesturing in supplication with her hands and murmuring so quietly that Nyssen strained to understand her, she no longer spoke to the people around her but to God alone:

> It is you, O Lord, who have freed us from the fear of death,
> you who have made the end of our life here the beginning of true life for us,
> you who put our bodies to rest in sleep a little while and will waken them again at the last trumpet,
> you who return our earth fashioned by your hands to the earth for safekeeping, and will retrieve again what you once gave, transforming what is mortal and unseemly in us with immortality and grace,
> you who have rescued us from the curse and from sin, having become both for our sakes,
>
> . . .
>
> O God the eternal one,
> to whom I have cleaved from my mother's womb
> whom my soul has loved with all its strength
> to whom I have dedicated my flesh and my soul from youth even until now,
> send an angel of light to be by my side to guide me to the place of refreshment, to the water of repose, in the bosom of the holy Fathers.
>
> . . .
>
> Do not let the terrible abyss sunder me from your elect
> or the Slanderer stand in the way to oppose me
> or my sin be uncovered before your eyes, if I have sinned in word or dead or thought, led astray in some way through the weakness of our nature.
> O you who have the power on earth to forgive sins, spare me that I may revive and as I put off my body be found before you without stain or blemish in the form of my soul.
> But may my soul be received into your hands, blameless and undefiled, as an incense offering in your sight.[29]

---

28. Gregory of Nyssa, *Life of Macrina* (trans. Silvas), 132–133.
29. Gregory of Nyssa, *Life of Macrina* (trans. Silvas), 133–135.

Completing her prayer, Marcina traced the sign of the cross over her eyes, mouth, and heart. Her mouth moved again, but her tongue had dried and her voice faded so that she no longer made any sound. In the twilight a lamp was brought into her room, and suddenly she opened her eyes wide and gazed toward the light. She wanted to sing the customary thanksgiving at the lighting of the lamps, perhaps the ancient hymn "Hail Gladdening Light." She could not voice the song but raised her hands and moved her lips. When she had given thanks in this way, she signed the cross once again over her face, "drew one more deep breath and with that brought to a close both her prayer and her life."[30]

In the stillness that followed, Nyssen remembered her instructions to give her body all the customary care. "So I reached out my hand, numbed with grief, to her holy face."[31] But her eyes were already closed and her whole body lay in natural repose, as if she had fallen asleep, lips at rest and hands over her breast.

The silence was quickly broken as wailing and crying rose from the sisters and Nyssen, too, gave himself up to lamentations. Clamor and chaos reigned for a time. At last, looking at Macrina's form, Nyssen knew that he must take up where she left off and lead in her stead. Raising his voice to be heard above the flood of anguished crying, he reminded the sisters that she had taught them to turn the passion of grief into prayer through psalmody. He then sent most of the women out to pray and sing psalms while he, Vetiana, and Lampadion, a deaconess appointed over the sisters of the monastery, set about preparing Macrina's body for the tomb.

These three soon discovered a point of difference in their efforts to honor Macrina. Nyssen wanted to reverence his sister by clothing her body in fine linen, but Vetiana explained that Macrina neither kept nor wanted finery, for she stored all her treasure in heaven. She had, in fact, no other clothing than the garment she wore. Lampadion was in tears as she told him, "The only adornment of concern to the holy one was a pure life. This was the ornament of her life and her shroud in death."[32] In gentle conversation, Vetiana yielded, perhaps moved by kindness toward a grieving brother, and perhaps feeling some comfort in this tribute to her beloved friend. She took the beautiful linen garments he offered and washed and dressed Macrina while Nyssen prepared for her funeral. As they worked,

---

30. Gregory of Nyssa, *Life of Macrina* (trans. Silvas), 136.
31. Gregory of Nyssa, *Life of Macrina* (trans. Silvas), 136.
32. Gregory of Nyssa, *Life of Macrina* (trans. Silvas), 138.

psalm-singing blended with lamentations outside, and people from the nearby farms and villages began filling the courtyard of the monastery.

When the preparations were finished, Lampadion gazed at the luminous beauty of Macrina arrayed in the fine linens and spoke up again, saying that it was simply "not fitting that she should be seen by the eyes of the virgins clothed as a bride."[33] She brought out an old, dark winter cloak that once belonged to Emmelia and suggested that Nyssen put it over her "so that this sacred beauty is not made to shine with an alien splendour of clothing."[34] And so, under her mother's dark robe, Macrina's hiddenness was carried right to the grave. Yet, even cloaked in this way, radiance illumined her body just as it had in Nyssen's dream. The fine raiment, although a loving tribute, was in the end superfluous to the grace that shone from the residue of Macrina's soul.

There followed an all-night vigil of prayer and hymn singing. As the vigil came to an end and the dawn prayer began, they heard the rising lamentations of men and women who had come in from the surrounding countryside. Nyssen drew these people into the funeral ceremony by placing women on one side and men on the other and leading them in "a single psalmody, rhythmical and harmonious, coming alternatively from either side as in choral singing, and blending beautifully in the common responses."[35]

As the day advanced, crowds of people kept coming so that the grounds were packed and there was no room to move. Nyssen and other priests in attendance, including a bishop named Araxius, lifted the bier for the procession to the family tomb, which lay about a mile from the monastery. They could move only very slowly, "for the people were pressing around the bier, all of them insatiable for that sacred sight, so that there was no way open for us to press on easily with the journey."[36] Deacons and attendants came up on either side carrying wax tapers in their hands, and "a kind of mystic procession was set in train, the psalmody resounding harmoniously from beginning to end."[37] The crowd kept growing as they went, gathering around, seeking closeness to the bier, and obstructing the way. The slow journey took almost the whole day.

---

33. Gregory of Nyssa, *Life of Macrina* (trans. Silvas), 142.
34. Gregory of Nyssa, *Life of Macrina* (trans. Silvas), 142.
35. Gregory of Nyssa, *Life of Macrina* (trans. Silvas), 143.
36. Gregory of Nyssa, *Life of Macrina* (trans. Silvas), 143.
37. Gregory of Nyssa, *Life of Macrina* (trans. Silvas), 144.

At the tomb, lamentations broke out again and there was disorder and confusion. With difficulty, Nyssen and the other priests restored order and continued the prayers. The tomb of their family was opened. Nyssen covered what was inside with a pure linen cloth to protect the dignity of their parents. Then he and Araxius lifted Macrina's body and laid her beside Emmelia, fulfilling the mutual request of mother and daughter.

According to her own teachings, in death Macrina was taken into the divine embrace, like Lazarus gathered into the bosom of Abraham. She arrived in her eternal home where she no longer requires food or drink, clothing or shelter, air or lamplight, where all her needs and hopes are met in God, who is her all in all.

Macrina described true freedom, saying, "freedom consists in reflecting the likeness of that which is without a master and is self-governing."[38] Turning modern preconceptions about virtue on their heads, she says that virtue and freedom are one and the same, which she explains in this way: Freedom is oneness with our own true nature. Divine likeness is our true nature, our essential character created by God (Gen 1:26–27) but lost through our unenlightened passions, disordered attachments, and errant choices. The divine is the essence and wellspring of good. Thus, freedom is returning to our true nature, which is reflecting the likeness of God, which is partaking in all that is good, which is virtue.

In bodiless life, Macrina is free of everything that might disrupt her immersion in the divine embrace. There is nothing to draw her away from a state of love for and in and with God. This state of love, she says, *is* the divine life. "This life is beautiful by nature and lovingly disposed by nature towards the beautiful and knows no limit to the activity of love."[39]

> For [the soul] has that which it hoped for, and being now wholly occupied in the enjoyment of the good . . . no other disposition is left to it now but that of love, which cleaves to the beautiful by natural affinity . . . When the soul therefore has become simple and one in form and accurately godlike, it finds that truly simple and immaterial good which alone is really loveable and desirable, and cleaves to it and is mingled with it through the movement and

---

38. Gregory of Nyssa, *On the Soul and the Resurrection* (trans. Silvas), 215.
39. Gregory of Nyssa, *On the Soul and the Resurrection* (trans. Silvas), 211.

activity of love, fashioning itself according to that which it is ever comprehending and discovering.[40]

Free, at one with her true created nature, and crossed over into eternal life, Macrina has only to partake of the limitless stream of blessings that flow from God. In this divine life, she is always growing, for the fountain of good never stops filling her and expanding her capacity to reflect the abundance and the power of divine beauty and love. This beauty and love, in turn, shine from her soul to illumine the way for those who contemplate her life and teachings, like light from a pure mirror turned to face the sun.

Meditation

Read over Macrina's prayer, or for Scripture meditation, consider 1 Cor 15:53–55, 2 Tim 4:6–8, Rom 8:38–39, and John 11:25–26. As we have practiced through the chapters of this small book, take time to still your body and mind. Read your chosen Scripture three times: for the words, for your response, and in readiness for any doors the spirit may open to you.

---

40. Gregory of Nyssa, *On the Soul and the Resurrection* (trans. Silvas), 210–11.

Epilogue

A Soldier's Tale

> "And immediately something like scales fell from his eyes, and his sight was restored. Then he got up and was baptized." (Acts 9:18)

NYSSEN STAYED AT ANNISA just long enough to complete all the funeral rites and arrangements, then he had to be on his way again, called to contend with various conflicts within the church. As he left the estate he visited the grave once more, "I cast myself on the tomb and embraced the dust, and so took to the road again, downcast and in tears, pondering how my life had been severed from so great a good."[1] Of his brief time with Macrina he wrote in Letter Nineteen:

> It was the same as a traveler at noon whose body is exhausted from the sun. He runs up to a spring, but alas, before he has touched the water, before he has cooled his tongue, all at once the stream dries up before his eyes and he finds the water turned to dust. So it was with me... I saw her whom I so longed to see... but before I could satisfy my longing, on the third day I buried her and returned on my way... Next, before I had digested this misfortune, the Galatians, who were neighbors of my church, having stealthily sown the sickness of the heresies usual among them in various localities of my church, provided me with no small struggle...[2]

---

1. Gregory of Nyssa, *Life of Macrina* (trans. Silvas), 145.
2. Gregory of Nyssa, "Letter Nineteen," 88–89.

EPILOGUE: A SOLDIER'S TALE

Nyssen stopped on his journey at the small city of Sebastopolis, where he met a military commander, related in some way to the family, who was stationed there with his troops. This man gave Nyssen a friendly greeting. When he heard of Macrina's death, he was dismayed. In tears, he told Nyssen a story.

The soldier and his wife had a little girl who developed a disease of the eyes so that "the membrane around her pupil was thickened and whitish."[3] The soldier's wife asked that they make a special visit to the school of thought and virtue, as he called Annisa, and so they went there.

At the monastery, the soldier went to the men's quarters and his wife and daughter to the women's to see Macrina. After they had visited a while, they felt they should take their leave, but as they were setting out Peter came to urge the soldier to join them at table, and Macrina cordially urged his wife and daughter eat with her.

> Holding our little daughter in her lap, she said she would not give her up until she had had a table prepared for them and had welcomed them with the bounty of philosophy. But when she kissed the child, as might be expected, she put her lips to her eyes, perceived the condition around the pupil, and said,
> "If you grant me this favour and share our table I will give in return a reward not unworthy of such honour on your part."
> "What is that?" said the child's mother.
> "I have a medicine," said the great one, "which is effective in healing eye complaints."[4]

Although concerned about the necessity of starting their journey home before nightfall, the soldier and his family were excited to feast and pray with the great teachers at the monastery. Peter and Macrina entertained them generously and sent them off, cheered and delighted, eagerly telling one another all about their experiences.

As the soldier's wife recounted every detail of what she saw and heard and did, she came to Macrina's promise of medicine and suddenly stopped. They had forgotten to bring away the medicine! The soldier, upset at their carelessness, was asking a servant to run back for the salve, but just then, "the infant, who was in her nurse's arms, looked at her mother, and the mother peered into the child's eyes."[5] She cried aloud in astonishment:

---

3. Gregory of Nyssa, *Life of Macrina* (trans. Silvas), 146.
4. Gregory of Nyssa, *Life of Macrina* (trans. Silvas), 146–47.
5. Gregory of Nyssa, *Life of Macrina* (trans. Silvas), 147.

> She really has given her own true medicine that heals diseases, the cure that comes from prayer, and it has already worked, and there is nothing more remaining of the eye's affliction. It has all been cleared up by that divine medicine![6]

The soldier's "voice kept breaking down in sobs and his tale overflowed with tears."[7] He thought of Jesus' miracles of giving sight to the blind, which he had not believed before. His daughter's eyes were healed through Macrina's faith, and his own spiritual sight was restored.

---

6. Gregory of Nyssa, *Life of Macrina* (trans. Silvas), 148.

7. Gregory of Nyssa, *Life of Macrina* (trans. Silvas), 148.

Appendix 1
Chapter Notes

Chapter One

Origen: While he was widely recognized as a genius, Origen's ideas were not universally accepted by his fellow Christians. In the words of John McGuckin, "his speculative mind stretched the boundaries of Christian thought and imagination in his own day and for generations after him."[1] His work had enormous influence and also generated enormous controversy, even hundreds of years after his death. Indeed, his teachings were condemned at the Fifth Ecumenical Council in 553 CE, and his writings banned and burned. However, "even after his condemnation he was too deeply inserted in the fabric of Christian theologizing ever to be dismissed or forgotten."[2]

Chapter Two

Problems of asceticism: A dualistic and hierarchical concept of reality seems to run through ascetic philosophies and to lead ascetics into difficulties. That is, even when they do not specifically say so, ascetics seem to work from an idea that our beings can be divided into two general kinds of nature and that one of these is better, or higher, than the other. People, the world, and the cosmos are thought of as divisible into mind and matter, or to put it

---

1. McGuckin, *Westminster Handbook to Origen*, 25.
2. McGuckin, *Westminster Handbook to Origen*, 26.

in other words, soul and body, the spiritual and the material, the philosophical and the tangible. Ascetics then try to place mind over matter, prioritize spiritual or philosophical aims over the drives and appetites of the body, and choose ideals of good over tangible rewards or advantages.

There is great beauty and nobility in the ascetic path. At same time, as we have seen, ascetics can follow their dualistic lines of thought to their logical conclusions and not only renounce privilege, power, and self-indulgence but actually reject the gift of embodied life itself. Almost every religious tradition has its examples of ascetic individuals, or whole orders, that have engaged in self-destructive and alarming practices. In what is perhaps an ironic demonstration of the very passions that ascetics hope to transcend, some ascetics seem to develop a lust for pain, a greed for self-denial, a pride in humiliation, a grandiosity of self-denigration. Disturbing and sad as these cases can be, the attraction of asceticism is based in longings that are at the core of human life—longings for freedom, justice, and fulfillment.

Jesus of Nazareth: Jesus lived and taught simplicity of life, but he was also known for eating, drinking, and feeding huge gatherings of people. In the Gospels, he invites his followers to feast again and again. His teaching is not about self-denial as an end in itself but rather as a release of attachments, freeing the Christian to live the Way and the truth.

Plato: Plato very explicitly articulated the dualistic hierarchical conceptualization.

Origen's ascetism: Origen saw the body as a necessary, although limited and problematic, vessel for the soul's work toward union with the divine. Unlike some later ascetics, he did not consider the body and its drives to be *evil* per se, but he saw them as a source of distraction from the soul's journey toward divine likeness.

Hydraulic: Readers of Freud may find interesting comparisons between Nyssen's hydraulic conception of human energies and Freud's drive theory.

Chapter Four

Plato: Whether Plato intended these arguments as his own final conclusions is a matter still debated by philosophers. He wrote in the form of dialogues in which his characters talk together as they try to clarify the nature of important concepts like justice, good, beauty, and the ideal city-state. In the dialogues, characters take different positions and develop their ideas.

As they reason through their thoughts, Plato's characters often change their minds, either because they are persuaded by what another speaker says or because they discover flaws in their own logic. Through this process, which Plato called dialectic, understanding or wisdom evolves. Plato does not tell the reader what to think but rather invites the reader to join in the dialectic, in the process of thinking. Thus, it is always important to keep in mind that arguments presented by Plato must be considered as invitations to question, discuss, and debate rather than as doctrines to be accepted.

Sheep: The original wild sheep and their early domestic descendants grew fur or hair, not wool—their coats were short and made up of coarse outer hairs and a soft underfur. In winter, the undercoat grew thick for warmth, and in spring the sheep molted, perhaps like a husky dog that grows a heavy, downy undercoat during the fall and then "blows" this underfur in a mass in spring. Hair-sheep were originally raised for meat and milk, as they still are in some traditional cultures in Africa as well as in industrialized countries. The earliest woolens were made from the underfur of these hair-sheep, which was not sheared, as are modern sheep, but gathered by hand-plucking and combing.

Fine wool: Of course, the finer the fabric desired, the more time-consuming its production. Using methods thought similar to those of the earliest sheep's wool producers, traditional Kashmiri women still comb cashmere wool from their goats and hand-sort the fibers before spinning. Ninety-four workdays are required to produce the wool for one fine garment![3]

Distaff and spindle: A distaff is a tool for keeping the combed, raw wool fibers ready for spinning. A drop spindle is, essentially, a stick with a specially formed weight. Archeological digs in the Near East have found fascinating examples of spindles, weights, and looms which show technological development in the design and manufacture of these important tools in early societies.

Chapter Five

Arguments both ways: Nyssen does not tell us what Macrina thought or felt about her planned betrothal, but his narrative makes clear that she needed to find a way to live out the destiny given in her secret name and thus to redeem her mother's sacrificed vocation. At the age of perhaps

3. McCorriston, "Fiber Revolution," 517–49.

thirteen, when her intended died, Macrina knew and felt this clearly enough to say that she intended to remain unmarried and dedicate her life to the pursuit of philosophy. She went on to carry out this decision with such clarity and unstinting commitment that it is hard to imagine that she ever felt any question in her heart. At the same time, however, she did live for perhaps one or two years with the necessity of obeying her father by marrying the man he chose.

When she learned of her father's plan, was it with a sense of disaster, of loss of her true calling? Did she pray, set her soul before God, ask for the strength to accept whatever God willed for her? Did she imagine herself married, imagine life with the young man, seek a sense of vocation in this? Did Macrina try to prepare herself to be spiritually joined in life with this man?

If he was Nazianzen's cousin Euphemius, or someone with similar qualities, perhaps she even felt some excitement about this prospect. It is unlikely that she knew him well, but she would have been told about him. If he spoke publicly, perhaps she saw and heard him. Possibly she was persuaded that being joined with him might become her way, her work, her calling. Then she was faced with his tragic and untimely death.

When her father talked to her about more men, other men, men wanting her for a wife, how could she contemplate such thing? Was her soul a commodity to be passed off from one man to another? It is easy to see how she would feel exactly the things that she said. If she had spiritually accepted a *marriage*, especially if this acceptance came at great cost and was specific to joining with *one* individual, how could anyone ask her to accept *another* different marriage? Rather, the death of her intended may have served to confirm and seal her commitment to her original calling. In this way, Macrina's insistence that she was a widow may have reflected both grief over the loss of her intended and an affirmed and deepened experience of the call to her vocation.

Chapter Six

God's likeness: Origen interpreted the two creation narratives in Genesis as containing both the idea of being created in the image of God and the idea of aspiring to achieve the likeness of God. Humans were *created in the image* of God in the first creation narrative in Genesis, while *we aspire to* *achieve likeness* with God, or spiritual union with the divine, through the soul's transformative and mystical journey.

Chapter Ten

Hades: Macrina goes on to say that, although it does not seem correct to her, she has no objection if other people prefer to think of Hades as an actual location where souls go after death. The important thing is that souls exist after life in the flesh has ended. She says, "location in a place is a property only of bodies," and so there is no reason to become involved, one way or the other, in arguments about whether souls are located in one place or another.

God becomes all in all: This section of interpretation closely follows this beautiful text from *On the Soul and the Resurrection*:

> For during our present life which is activated in varied and diverse conditions, we partake of many things, such as time and air and place, both food and drink, and clothing, and sunlight, and lamp-light, and many other necessities of life, none of which is god. That blessedness to which we look forward however has no need of any these things, because the divine nature will become to us and replace all, dispensing itself harmoniously to every need of that life. This is surely clear from the divine sayings, that for those who are deserving God becomes place (cf. John 14:2–3) and house (cf. Eph 2:19–22) and clothing (cf. Matt 22:11–12, Gal 3:27) and food and drink (cf. John 6:35, 48–58) and light (cf. Ps 26:1, 33:6, 118:105, John 8:1) and riches (cf. Luke 12:21, Rom 9:23, Eph 1:8, 2:7) and dominion (cf. Matt 5:3, 5:10, 19:28, Luke 12:32) and everything conceivable and namable that contributes to the good life for us.[4]

---

4. Gregory of Nyssa, *On the Soul and the Resurrection* (trans. Silvas), 216.

Appendix 2
Timeline

As noted in the introduction, most of the dates provided here are uncertain to one degree or another. In reading various scholarly works, differing dates are often found, and conflicting accounts of facts and sequences of events are also common. I have tried to rely on well-researched, up-to-date sources, but the dates here are approximations intended to aid the reader in following the people and events of Macrina's story.

Year (CE)

184	Birth Origen
213	Birth Thaumaturgus
250's	All subjects required to sacrifice to Roman Gods or be imprisoned/executed
251	Birth of St. Anthony of the Desert (upper Egypt, 1/12/251)
253	Death Origen
260?	Birth St. Macrina the Elder
270	Death Thaumaturgus
270 (285?)	St. Anthony of the Desert follows Matthew 19:21, gives away his wealth, goes into solitude

APPENDIX 2: TIMELINE

293 (296,298)	Birth of St. Athanasius, biographer of St. Anthony of Desert
295?	Birth Basil the Elder
303	Edict of persecution under Diocletian begins the Great Persecution
305–309?	Birth Emmelia (making her 18 to 22 at Macrina's birth and 61 to 65 at death)
313	Emperor Constantine's Edict of Milan legalizes Christianity in the empire and ends the Great Persecution
324	Constantine sole ruler
	Soon after assuming power, Constantine begins the construction of Constantinople.
325	Council of Nicaea called by Constantine, attended by 250 to 318 bishops, plus two priests and three deacons for each bishop, for a total of around 1500. Constatine invited all 1800 bishops of the Christian church (1000 in East and 800 in West). Attendees included Eusebius of Caesarea, Alexander of Alexandria (Bishop), and Athanasius of Alexandria (then a young deacon). This council produced the Nicene Creed which is still recited today.
326?	Marriage Emmelia and Basil the Elder
327	Birth Macrina
329	Birth Basil
330	Constantinople inaugurated the new Capital of Rome.
330 (331?)	Birth Naucratius
335	Birth Gregory (Nyssen)
	(Marcina's 4 sisters born somewhere in here, one brother is born and perishes)
337	Death Constantine, Constantinius II rules the East
339	Macrina turns 12, betrothal planned
340	Death St. Macrina the Elder (Macrina 13)

APPENDIX 2: TIMELINE

340 or 341?	Death Macrina's intended
344?	Earthquake in Neocaesaria? (Macrina 17)
345	Death Basil the Elder (Macrina 18)
	Birth of Peter
	Move to Anissa
347	Macrina turns 20
349	Basil departs for Constantinople to study under Libanius
350	Basil goes to study in Athens
351	Naucratius wows the public with his speaking gift (Basil still in Athens)
	Naucratius age 21 or 22 vows to the ascetic life and goes into hermitage
356	(Spring) Death Naucratius
	Basil rather suddenly returns after 6 years in Athens, possibly due to Naucratius's death
	Basil briefly practices law and teaches rhetoric in Caesarea
356?	Basil sets aside his legal and teaching aspirations to devote his life to God
	Death St. Anthony of Desert (1/12/356, age 105).
	Athanasius, who is between 58 and 63, probably starts working on The Life of St. Anthony around this time.
357	Basil travels to Egypt, Palestine, Syria, and Mesopotamia to study ascetics and monasticism.
358	Basil returns from his travels
	Basil (29) and Peter (13-ish) establish a men's monastic community at Annisa parallel to Macrina's already thriving women's community
360	Basil leaves the retreat at Annisa to travel to Synod of Constantinople
	Basil and Athanasius correspond in anti-Arian efforts

APPENDIX 2: TIMELINE

361	Death Constantius II, Julian the Apostate becomes emperor
362	Peter vows to ascetic life
363	Basil returns to Annisa where Macrina's and Peter's monastic communities continue
	Death Emperor Julian, Valens becomes emperor.
368	The great draught and famine (Basil's Homily on The Famine and Drought)
	The City of Nicaea almost destroyed by earthquake.
370	Basil succeeds to See of Caesarea
371	Death Emmelia
	Basil ordains Peter (age 26) to the Priesthood
372	(January) Valens's visit and confrontation with Basil
	Basil consecrates Gregory (Nyssen) as Bishop of Nyssa
	(September) Roman Census, Cappadocia is divided in two, Caesarea becomes the only city in newly-created Cappadocia Prima. Basil is Metropolitan with no subordinates and many notables are transferred to Tyana, capital of new the province of Cappadocia Secunda.
378	Death Emperor Valens, Theodosius becomes Emperor of the East
	Cappadocia reunited as one province
	Death Basil (age 49)
379	Death Macrina (age 52)
382	Cappadocia divided again
392	Death Emperor Theodosius
395	Death Nyssen (age 60)

Bibliography

Adamson, Peter, and Ganeri, Jonardon. *A History of Philosophy Without Any Gaps: Classical Indian Philosophy*. Oxford: Oxford University Press, 2020.
Alter, Robert. *The Hebrew Bible Vol. 1, The Five Books of Moses*. New York: W. W. Norton, 2019.
Athanasius of Alexandria. *Life of St. Anthony of Egypt*. Translated by Philip Schaff and Henry Wace. Pantionos Classics, 2021.
Basil of Caesarea. *The Complete Works of Saint Basil*. Translated by Philip Schaff. Toronto: Public Domain, Amazon Kindle, 2016.
———. "The Hexaemeron." In Basil of Caesarea, *The Complete Works of Saint Basil*. Toronto: Public Domain, Amazon Kindle, 2016.
———. "In Time of Famine and Drought." In Susan Holman, *The Hungry Are Dying: Beggars and Bishops in Roman Cappadocia*. Oxford: Oxford University Press, 2020.
———. "In Time of Famine and Drought." In C. Paul Schroeder, *On Social Justice: St. Basil the Great*. Yonkers, NY: St. Vladimir's Seminary Press, 2008.
———. "Letter 93, To the Patrician Caesaria, Concerning Communion." In Basil of Caesarea, *The Complete Works of Saint Basil* (Loc 7452–59). Toronto: Public Domain, Amazon Kindle, 2016.
———. "Letter 210, To the Learned in Neocaesarea." In Anna Silvas, *Macrina the Younger: Philosopher of God*, 73–75. Turnhout: Brepolis, 2008.
———. "The Long Rules." In Basil of Caesarea, *The Complete Works of Saint Basil*. Toronto: Public Domain, Amazon Kindle, 2016.
———. *Saint Basil Collection*. Philadelphia: Aerterna, 2015.
Bauer, Susan Wise. *The History of the Ancient World: From the Earliest Accounts to the Fall of Rome*. New York: W. W. Norton, 2007.
Breniquet, Catherine. "Functions and Uses of Textiles in the Ancient Near East, Summary and Perspectives." In *Textile Production and Consumption in the Ancient Near East: Archeology, Epigraphy, Iconography*, edited by Marie-Louise Nosch, et al. 1–25. Oxford: Oxbow, 2013.

Breniquet, Catherine, and Michel, Cecile. "Wool Economy in the Ancient Near East and the Aegean." In *Wool Economy in the Ancient Near East and the Aegean*, edited by Catherine Breniquet and Cecile Michel, 14–35. Oxford: Oxbow, 2014.

Gregory of Nazianzus. *Saint Gregory Nazianzen Collection*, Aeterna. Amazon Kindle, 2016.

Gregory of Nyssa. *On the Soul and the Resurrection*. Translated by C. P. Roth. Crestwood: St. Vladimir's Seminary Press, 1993.

———. *The Life of Saint Macrina*. Translated by Kevin Corrigan. Eugene: Wipf and Stock, 2005.

———. "Letter Nineteen." In Anna Silvas, *Macrina the Younger, Philosopher of God*, translated by Anna Silvas, 83–92. Turnhout: Brepolis, 2008.

———. "On the Soul and the Resurrection." In Anna Silvas, *Macrina the Younger, Philosopher of God*, translated by Anna Silvas, 171–246. Turnhout: Brepolis, 2008.

———. "The Life of Macrina." In Anna Silvas, *Macrina the Younger, Philosopher of God*, translated by Anna Silvas, 109–138. Turnhout: Brepolis, 2008.

———. "On the Making of Man." In Gregory of Nyssa, *Saint Gregoy of Nyssa Collection*, translated by Philip Schaff. Aeterna. Retrieved from http://www.aerternapress.com.

———. *Saint Gregory of Nyssa Collection*. Aeterna. Amazon Kindle, 2016.

———. "On Virginity." In *On Virginity by St. Gregory of Nyssa, St. Clement of Rome and St. Ambrose*, translated by Anna Skoubourdis, 9–63. Jerusalem: St. George Monastery, 2020.

———. *The Life of Gregory the Wonderworker*. http://www.documentacatholicaomnia.eu/03d/0330-0395,_Gregorius_Nyssenus,_The_Life_Of_Gregory_The_Wonderworker_EN.doc

Henderson, Jeffrey, ed. *The Greek Anthology* (Vol. II, Book VIII), translated by W. R. Patton. London: Loeb Classical Library, 1917.

Holman, Susan R. *The Hungry Are Dying: Beggars and Bishops in Roman Cappadocia*. New York: Oxford University Press, 2001.

Lumb, David. "Textiles, Value, and the Early Economies of North Syria and Anatolia." In *Textile Production and Consumption in the Ancient Near East: Archeology, Epigraphy, Iconography*, edited by Marie-Louise Nosch, Henriette Koefoed, and Eva Andersson Strand, 54–77. Oxford: Oxbow, 2013.

McCorriston, Joy. "The Fiber Revolution." *Current Anthropology* (1997) 517–49.

McGuckin, John Anthony, ed. *The Westminster Handbook to Origen*. Louisville: Westminster John Knox, 2004.

Meister, Chad, and J. B. Stump. *Christian Thought: A Historical Introduction* (2nd ed.). New York: Routledge, 2017.

Origen of Alexandria. "De Principiis." In Origen of Alexandria, *The Complete Works of Origen*. Toronto: Public domain, Amazon Kindle, 2016.

———. *The Complete Works of Origen*. Toronto: Public domain via Amazon Kindle, 2016.

Plato. *Plato, Collected Dialogues, Including the Letters* (E. A. Hamilton, ed.). Princeton: Princeton University Press, 1961.

———. Republic. In Plato, *The Collected Dialogues including the Letters*, translated by P. Shorey, 575–844. Princeton: Princeton University Press, 1980.

———. *Theaetetus*. In Plato, *The Collected Dialogues including the Letters*, translated by F. M. Cornford, 845–919). Princeton: Princeton University Press, 1980.

Schaff, Phillip. "Sketch of the Life and Works of Saint Basil." In Basil of Caesarea, *The Complete Works of Saint Basil*. Toronto: Public Domain, Amazon Kindle, 2016.

Schroeder, C. Paul. *St. Basil the Great on Social Justice.* Yonkers, New York: St. Vladimir's Seminary Press, 2009.

Silvas, Anna. *Macrina the Younger, Philosopher of God.* Turnhout: Brepolis, 2008.

St. Clement of Rome (attributed to). "Epistles On Virginity." In Gregory, St. Clement, & Ambrose, *On Virginity*, translated by Anna Skoubourdis, & Monaxi Agapi, 64–86. Jerusalem: St. George Monastery, 2020.

Strand, Eva Anderson. "Sheep, Wool and Textile Production. An Interdisciplinary Approach to the Complexity of Wool Working." In *Wool Economy in the Ancient Near East and the Aegean,* edited by Catherine Breniquet and Cecile Michel, 91–112. Oxford: Oxbow, 2014.

The Acts of Paul and Thecla. Translated by Jeremiah Jones. Kerry: CrossReach, 2019.

The Sayings of the Desert Fathers. Translated by Benedicta Ward. Oxford: A. R. Mowbray, 1975.

Thomason, Allison Karmel. "Her Share of the Profits: Women, Agency, and Textile Production at Kultepe/Kanesh in the Early Second Millennium BC." In *Textile Production and Consumption in the Ancient Near East: Archeology, Epigraphy, Iconography*, edited by Marie-Louise Nosch, Henriette Koefoed, and Eva Andersson Strand, 93–112. Oxford: Oxbow, 2013.

Van Dam, Raymond. *Kingdom of Snow.* Philadelphia: University of Pennsylvania Press, 2002.

———. *Families and Friends in Late Roman Cappadocia.* Philadelphia: University of Pennsylvania Press, 2003.

www.ingramcontent.com/pod-product-compliance
Lightning Source LLC
Chambersburg PA
CBHW072153160426
43197CB00012B/2361